FROM
MULTIPLE HINDU GODS
TO
One God

FROM MULTIPLE HINDU GODS TO
One God

A Girl's Journey

MAMTA MUKERJEE

XULON PRESS

Xulon Press
2301 Lucien Way #415
Maitland, FL 32751
407.339.4217
www.xulonpress.com

Paperback ISBN-13: 978-1-66285-267-1
Ebook ISBN-13:978-1-66285-268-8

Table of Contents

Endorsements. ix

Acknowledgements xv

Dedication. xvii

Prologue. xix

Chapter 1. Near-Death Experience. 1

Chapter 2. Childhood Memories. .7

Chapter 3. Who to Trust, Gods or Faith Healers? 11

Chapter 4. Faith versus Fear. 17

Chapter 5. Depression. 23

Chapter 6. Coming to America.. 27

Chapter 7. My Church Invitation. .35

Chapter 8. Long Awaited Prayers Answered.. 39

Chapter 9. A New Life Without Church. 45

Chapter 10. Uncertainties and Unknown Future. 49

Chapter 11. My Culprit Was Finally Revealed.. 55

Chapter 12. Downward Spiral of My Life. 59

Chapter 13. Embarked on the Path of Lord Krishna.. 67

Chapter 14. Bittersweet Visit to Michigan. 75

Chapter 15. A Dead-End in My Life. 83

Chapter 16. Reunion with Bindu. .89

Chapter 17. My Struggle to Accept Jesus. 95

Chapter 18. Divine Encounter with Jesus. 105

Chapter 19. Water Baptism. 111

Chapter 20. My Initial Walk with Jesus. 115

Chapter 21. Golden Keys to Unlock the Healing. 121

    Be a Good Steward of God's Word. 123

    Confession, Repentance, and Forgiveness. 126

    Fight Offensively. 130

    Acknowledging Our Hurts and Pains. 133

    Breaking Self-Imposed and Others' Curses. 140

    Reject Ungodly Thoughts.. 144

    Become the Warrior God Has Called Us to Be. 147

Epilogue. 153

About the Author. 157

Endorsements

Mamta lives and breathes the Gospel of Jesus Christ. She has the perfect redemption story of being the one whom Jesus turned aside to look for and save. He healed and delivered her and gave her a passion for life with Him. Her story and her life will reach many with the testimony of how Jesus saves, heals, and delivers. I'm continually inspired by her daily walk with Jesus as she helps people encounter Him and His healing power.

~ **Annie Blouin**, author of
Reaganista, Everlasting Doors: When the Supernatural Penetrates American Politics, Everlasting Prophetic: Bridging Heaven to Earth, and Prophetic Revelation: Keys to Spiritual Maturity

Have you ever desperately searched for healing? Or needed a miracle that couldn't be obtained through normal channels? As Mamta shared about her Hindu beliefs and culture along with her amazing stories, I not only enjoyed reading her book but I LOVED reading about her desperate journey to find the highest God in all kinds of places. In fact, He already knew her and her needs, and was lovingly drawing her to Himself. So reader, open your heart and get ready to discover this highest God for yourself... to hope, to be healed and to taste and see that the Lord is good!

~ **Barbara Koob,** speaker, teacher,
and author of the book "Dream Discoveries -
Learn to Hope and Dream with Purpose"

I highly recommend this read! Mamta's personal conversion from Hinduism to born-again believer in Jesus Christ, is a very riveting story that captivated me from the first page to the last. The power of redemption through Jesus Christ is in full view for the reader. No other religion has a God who is alive and well on the planet earth. The power to save, heal and deliver is revealed in the person of Jesus Christ.
Mamta's story is proof of that.

~ **Christy Christopher** Author/Speaker
www.christineachristopher.com

This is a thoroughly enjoyable and satisfying book, detailing Mamta's personal journey to find religious meaning and healing through Jesus Christ. This first-time author uses a masterful writing style to help the reader better understand what was most important in her thought process as we effortlessly follow the challenges of her journey. She grabs our attention immediately, describing her harrowing experience on the streets of New Delhi. But most importantly, Mamta adds credibility that most people (Christians and non-Christians alike) will relate to, as she skillfully describes each step along the way to her conversion. Her words clearly reflect the many questions she had and the answers she needed to make this happen, and having it happen over a period of many years makes for a much more realistic and compelling story than simply going from point A to point B.

~ **Robert Russo**
Former Communications Director

ENDORSEMENTS

In Mamta Mukerjee's new book, "From Multiple Hindu Gods to One God, A Girl's Journey," Mamta takes the reader on a journey of faith from Delhi, India to the United States. Mamta presents a compelling case for a life healed emotionally and physically by Jesus Christ. Coming to Jesus as a Hindu requires radical obedience and courage. Mamta shows the reader how to trust in a loving God when the risks are high.

~ **Dr. Nick Gough, MTS, D.Min**
Former Senior Pastor at Hope Chapel, Apex, NC
Author of "When the Old Becomes New"

Mamta asked me to read her book, "From Multiple Hindu gods to One God" and share with her my thoughts. My plan was to read three chapters a day until I finished. However, I did not follow my plan. Once I finished the third chapter I couldn't stop reading. So, I kept reading until I finished that very evening.

This inspiring book tells Mamta's amazing story of how she journeyed from being a devout Hindu to a born-again believer and disciple of the Lord Jesus Christ. Her hunger for freedom from depression and anxiety brought her to her healing at the feet of the Lord Jesus. Her book also tells the story of her amazing God that was reaching out to her as she was seeking Him. It is His story of incredible love, grace, and power.

I know you will be blessed and inspired by reading this book.

~ **Richard Dial**
Former Lead Pastor of Cary Church of God
Currently Church Plant Missionary to Ecuador

When Mamta first contacted me about writing an endorsement for her book, From Multiple Hindu gods to One God, I was so busy I almost turned her down. After reading her book, I am so glad that I didn't miss the opportunity. Mamta's book grabs you from the very first chapter with the miraculous power of God to rescue us. I was on the edge of my seat throughout the entire book anticipating what would happen next.

Mamta's book tells an amazing story of the One True God who longs to have a relationship with us. Her testimony reveals how Jesus pursued her diligently until she came to the full knowledge of Him as her Savior. I would encourage you to read this book and share it with a friend who does not know Christ as their Lord and Savior.

I was not able to put the book down until I finished reading it. Mamta has such a genuine transparency that reveals just how loving and kind Our Savior is, and how desperately He wants to do the miraculous in our lives.

You will be inspired by how God healed Mamta physically, and moved powerfully in her life. I imagine you will also have a hard time putting the book down.

~ **Donna Sparks** - Assemblies of God Evangelist, Author of *"Beauty from Ashes: My Story of Grace," "No Limits: Embracing the Miraculous,"* and *"The Masquerade: Deception in The Last Days,"* Podcast Host, and Founder and Director of Story of Grace Prison Ministry www.DonnaSparks.com

ENDORSEMENTS

From Multiple Hindu gods to One God, a girl's journey, by Mamta Mukerjee, is a remarkable telling of the author's journey from sickness to healing, from youth to adulthood and, most importantly, from Hinduism to the saving grace of Jesus Christ. Mukerjee's honesty in this book will touch your heart as she reveals the struggles she faced with her health over many years and the disappointments of her search for healing through worship of Hindu gods, faith healers, and even traditional western medicine. But God had a hold on her heart before she even realized it and her faith came to be fulfilled with healing and peace. Her bold testimonies about her transformation and her love of Jesus will captivate you as she tells her story.

~ **Nancy Wakeley**, Author of gold medal winning
Heirloom: A Kate Tyler novel, contributor to *9/11: That Beautiful Broken Day* and her upcoming book,
The Legend, A Kate Tyler novel

Acknowledgements

I first want to thank my friend, Judy Russo, for coming forth, putting in endless effort, and taking her precious time in editing the contents of this book. Without her insightfulness and clarity, I wouldn't have been able to convey my story in the meticulous manner in which it is written. I thank her for encouraging me to keep going, challenging me to take a pause at times, and helping me put my story in perspective. Judy is truly a gift from God!

I thank God too, for bringing me Madelyn Hamby, a UNC Chapel Hill graduate, just when I needed her. A stranger for only moments, Madelyn jumped on board and became my proofreader.

I thank my husband, Shobu Mukerjee, for pushing me along and making me persevere, so that I could finish writing what I started. When I forgot some of the most relevant events in my life, he reminded and inspired me to include them in my book. I admire him for his timely help and guidance.

Thank you to those from the Body of Christ who prayed for me and spoke blessings over this book from its conception to birth as a published book.

Dedication

With a grateful heart, I dedicate this book to my Lord and Savior, Jesus Christ, under whose scribe anointing, insight, and wisdom I was able to write my personal story. About four years ago, Jesus put a strong desire in my heart to share His testimony of my life with the world, and He gave me all that I needed to give birth to this book by His revelation and inspiration.

I thank my wonderful husband, Shobu, for supporting me every step of the way on this journey of writing and publishing the book. He has witnessed the positive changes, healing, deliverance, and blessings the Lord has brought into my life. This is why he has made ways for me to serve and honor the Lord!

Last of all, I would like to leave behind the footprint for my two beautiful daughters, Anita and Mia. Over the past decade, both have developed their love for Jesus and have witnessed His miraculous power working in their own young lives.

Prologue

*N*ever in my wildest imagination would I have thought that I would, or even could, make a transition from a devout Hindu to a born-again believer and follower of Christ. *What made me take the drastic step of divorcing my Hindu gods and goddesses, who I adored and worshipped for so long, to accept Christ as my Lord and Savior? What convinced me that Jesus, the God of Christianity, is the Way, the Truth, and the Life for all people, regardless of race, nationality, or background?*

John 14:6-7 (New International Version - NIV)

Jesus answered, "I am the way and the truth and the life. No one comes to the Father except through me. If you really know me, you will know my Father as well. From now on, you do know him and have seen him."

This book not only takes you through my spiritual journey, but answers the questions above as well as some that people have asked me over the years. I wrote it simply to share the goodness and attributes of my Lord and Savior, Jesus Christ, and to encourage those who are seeking. I was spiritually and physically broken. Without Jesus coming into my life and giving me a chance to be reborn into His divine family, I would never have enjoyed the good health I have to this day. I am here today on this beautiful planet only because of Dr. Jesus, *THE* Great Physician!

God knew me from the moment I was conceived in my mother's womb. It was no mistake I was born into the Hindu religion and enthusiastically served many Hindu gods and goddesses. My formative years, growing up in a loving family, exposed me to all the Hindu religion has to offer: its gods, traditions, rituals, and culture. Although Hindu gods couldn't cure me of my physical ailments, God nevertheless blessed me with an opportunity to enjoy the richness, treasures, and knowledge the Hindu religion bestowed upon me. I am thankful for that.

Along with my family, I practiced Hinduism religiously for decades. My Hindu beliefs were first challenged at the age of thirteen when I began to experience physical and emotional agony. I suffered from depression, throbbing headaches, hair loss, hypothyroidism, infertility, insomnia, hyperpigmentation, recurring painful mouth blisters, and Celiac disease. In addition to Western medicine, I sought the help of holistic medicine, but none of these paths brought relief to my pain or healed these infirmities.

I gradually ventured out seeking relief from other spiritual religious paths including Sikhism, god Krishna (Hare Rama Hare Krishna), and the teachings of Indian gurus and saints. In desperation, I reached out to faith healers, a common practice among locals in India. Their powerful spiritual insight and healing power convinced me to believe in them and have faith that they would save me. But this turned out to be a dangerous path, and I became entangled in mysticism on more than one occasion before I learned my lesson.

The book invites you to peek into my complex thirty-year journey with all its heartaches, roadblocks, and dead ends. But with God's grace and intervention, it didn't end there. There was an immediate turn around when I surrendered my life into the hands of Jesus and invited Him into my heart. This is the story of an ordinary girl whose life was transformed after a supernatural encounter with *THE* Extraordinary God, Jesus Christ of Nazareth!

Chapter 1
Near-Death Experience

*E*ven to this day, every time I think of that horrific accident on New Delhi's busiest highway, I shiver with goosebumps and chills.

About twelve years ago, I took my young daughters, then aged five and eight, for the very first time from the United States to my birthplace. Despite the warnings about Delhi not being as safe as it was when I grew up, I was thrilled to be in my home country again. I was beyond excited to introduce my children to India, my mom, and the rest of the family. That excitement was paramount in my mind, but a near-death experience that I have re-lived many times has since replaced many of the good memories from that visit.

It was a cold, December night, and I was out shopping with my mom and daughters at one of the many crowded and colorful bazaars (markets) of Delhi. There was a sea of people, almost shoulder to shoulder, and a myriad of things to see, touch, and taste. Mom and I made sure to keep a close eye on our girls and hold them tight to keep them near and safe. I knew about children being snatched away from their inattentive parents, so we were cautious but not fearful.

After our shopping adventure, my mom helped me find an auto rickshaw (a small motor vehicle with three wheels) and asked the driver in Hindi (Indian language) to take us back to our hotel. Before we parted, we hugged and said our goodbyes, even as we were already looking forward to the next day's adventure. I tucked the girls inside the covered side of the rickshaw, while I snuggled up against them from the outer, open-ended side. We were tired but relaxed, and I loved seeing the delight in my children's eyes as we reminisced about our wonderful day.

Traffic, as usual, was heavy and congested that night with all sorts of vehicles traveling at varying speeds between 30 and 60 miles per hour. Of course, bikes and manual rickshaws were the slowest and at the mercy of cars, buses, and trucks that had to maneuver around them at higher speeds. In India, it is common for drivers to ignore the traffic rules. Without using turn signals, they just honk their horns loudly to tell other drivers they need space to go around or change lanes. It's a noisy affair and traffic jams are common in Delhi.

We had been traveling about four miles when I saw a motorcycle come out of nowhere and pull parallel to our rickshaw. It was so close I could almost touch the motorcyclist. It didn't dawn on me until later that one of the handles of my purse was hanging out in the open, no doubt enticing the thieves. While the driver kept the motorcycle steady, the passenger in the seat behind him managed to grab hold of the dangling handle of my purse.

Each time he yanked it harder and harder, it sent a searing ring of fire around my wrist. Our passports were in my purse; I was not going to let it go. The thieves were adamant in their mission, but I persevered through fear and pain just as stubbornly. I held onto the metal bar of the rickshaw firmly to keep me in and bolster my strength in fighting them off. With each assault, I felt my grip loosening. This tug of war went on for about ten minutes. My driver had no way to help me or to deter the thieves, as he navigated through the traffic which dictated his speed. My kids screamed and cried uncontrollably. When I thought I couldn't endure it any longer, something even more dreadful happened.

With one last powerful jolt, the thief managed to wrench me from my seat. I flew out of the rickshaw and landed hard, face down on the rough patchwork of asphalt, still tethered to him by the strap of my purse. The kids watched in horror, as I was being dragged behind the motorcycle. The glasses flew off my face and instantly, the world around me became frightful and everything hazed over. The flashing lights and glare from headlights of oncoming traffic disoriented and blinded me. Now the thieves zoomed ahead even faster leaving the rickshaw behind, as they finagled their way through the moving vehicles. I screamed for help, but my voice evaporated somewhere in the din of the traffic. The city air was blanketed with smog, and the poisonous exhaust from motorized vehicles almost suffocated me.

With each quick change of the driver's direction as he weaved through traffic, my head slammed from side to side, and my face scraped from every bump and crevice on the road. As my body hit dirty potholes, I felt the splash of stagnant water on me. I was pummeled by stones and debris on the highway, while I was dragged along the rutted asphalt. My legs fishtailed this way and that in the opposite direction of my head, as they trailed behind uselessly. I could feel my heart pounding as though it would burst out from my chest. Blood was stinging my eyes, and my lips and mouth were sore and dry. There seemed no end to my suffering and no end to the thieves' malicious intent.

I began to panic as anxious thoughts swarmed through my mind. I couldn't turn my head to see my young children, but I knew they were now at the mercy of a complete stranger - a stranger who knew no English. *How much longer was I to endure this hell?* I couldn't know it at the time, but this hell I was enduring nearly paled by comparison to the next terrifying episode that was in store for me.

In a flash, the motorcyclists gave up the fight and let go of the strap that leashed me to them! They sped forward, leaving me in the middle of the highway with traffic swirling around. I was now untethered and thus *more* vulnerable, an easy target for the mass of vehicles heading straight toward me, as I lay helpless, unable to move, and unable to crawl. There was nothing to protect me and nowhere to escape. I felt certain I would be hit and crushed by the next coming vehicle. The thieves had left me for dead.

My mind went blank; I laid motionless, face down. I had nothing left to fight. Suddenly, something strong and deliberate scooped me up from the road and lifted me into the air. *Was I hit? Was I killed?* In one quick motion, *our* driver brought me back into *our* rickshaw next to my very own children! *"How could he have done this while driving?"; "How did he appear at just the right moment?"* It seemed like a dream. I hugged my children, and I remember clearly hearing the sweet sound of our driver's voice consoling the children in his native tongue. It was later I learned that the driver hadn't let me out of his sight after I was pulled from his rickshaw. He had been following from behind the entire time I was being dragged along the streets of Delhi. *This stranger saved my life!*

I must have been in shock, but I do remember giving the driver my mom's address. My next recollection was him stopping at Mom's house. He called her out and explained what I had just been through. He comforted me, as he patiently waited for my mom and sister to gather their things and acquire a second auto rickshaw to rush me to the emergency room of the nearest hospital.

As soon as we arrived at the ER, I was lifted onto a stretcher and taken immediately into an examination room. More than one doctor examined me concurrently from head to toe, and I could hear them ordering tests: an MRI Brain Scan for my head injuries and X-rays to locate fractured bones and joint dislocations. I remember being hooked up to an IV, given narcotics for the pain, and watching the nurses clean, treat my wounds, and tending to the contusions I suffered.

The worst pain at that moment was a pounding headache, causing intense pressure in my temples as though I was still being hammered on the highway. My teeth and jaw were painful to the touch. But I was alive. I was intact. My precious children were finally brought back to me. When the attendants lifted me onto a hospital bed, I continued to ruminate about the events I had just endured, reliving the fear and trauma over and over in my mind. I was grateful when the effects of the pain and sleeping medication overcame me, and I drifted into sleep.

The following morning, when I woke up, I knew where I was and why. My whole body was sore and with each pain, I recalled the events of the previous night. The nurse checked my vital signs again and the doctor, who entered the room, shared the good news of the medical report. I could see the surprise on his face when he told me what the tests revealed: no bones were broken, no concussion, no internal bleeding, and no injury to my brain. Other than bruises, scrapes, and wounds, I was fine. Although the doctor didn't speak the words, his facial expression was clear: *This was a miracle!* I was released from the hospital that morning and was advised to rest for the next few days.

Resting time gave me an opportunity to ponder the accident and the fact that my children and I survived relatively unscathed. It was clear that someone was watching over us. *No, not watching us; standing by us. No, it was more than that; it was as though this "angel of mercy" stood ready to intervene at the right moment.* I didn't know *THE ONE* God at that time, but it wasn't necessary to know everything just yet. Nevertheless, this wretched experience transcended me to some level of understanding of which I had been ignorant. I was certain someone all-powerful, all-knowing, and all-present had delivered me from the clutches of my enemies and spared the lives of my children. We were protected from harm without any awareness, and I knew that what I had been searching for was real. I saw the rickshaw driver as a *"sent angel"* and began to wonder *who* sent *him.*

This was a *turning* point. The ordeal that could have terminated me instead lifted me up on the path to find *who* rescued us that night. And thus my journey really began back in India, the country of my birth, where I worshiped many gods and dutifully prayed to idols who couldn't hear or see me. I had a lot more searching to do before I found *THE ONE* God in January of 2011, but when I did encounter Him, there was no mistaking it.

Chapter 2
Childhood Memories

*M*any years ago, I was born into a Hindu family in New Delhi, the capital city of India that never sleeps. The two cities, Old and New Delhi, are within the same state; there is no border differentiating the two. Old Delhi portrays the soul of Delhi, and it gives us a glimpse of how Delhi used to be during the Mughal reign. It is famous for its historical buildings including Lal Qila (Mughal Fort), Jama Masjid (mosque), Jain Mandir (Hindu temple), Sis Ganj Sahib Gurudwara (Sikh temple), and Raj Ghat (burial memorial of Mahatma Gandhi). It is home to Chandni Chowk – the oldest, busiest, and most famous market in all of India.

New Delhi, on the other hand, is a metropolitan city. It has high-rise buildings, extensive metro facilities, and all the amenities and luxuries one could think of. The important and impressive buildings include India Gate (formerly known as the All-India War Memorial) which was built in 1921, Parliament House constructed between 1921-1927, Rashtrapati Bhavan (official residence of the Indian President) built in 1931, and many more structures built by the British, which have all been well maintained. What a privilege to be born and raised in the hustle and bustle of a multicultural and vibrant city like New Delhi!

I am the first-born child of my lovely parents who absolutely adored me and my two sisters. I was born on Valentine's Day, so my parents named me Mamta, *which means love.* My mom, who recently passed away, had always been a housewife and a close friend to many. Full of earthly wisdom, knowledge, and understanding, she was the kind of woman who others sought out for a listening ear. She believed there is a god who can meet us wherever we are in life. Although my mother stayed away from idolatry and ceremony, she was quick to consult and adopt any spiritual guru, saint, or faith healer's advice to overcome obstacles that might arise in her life.

Mom was the strong pillar of our house and a warrior woman who was determined to fight until the end for a worthy cause. She was intentional in her pursuits, courageous, resolute, and full of encouragement. Time and again, I saw her stand strong during the trials and tribulations of our family. This attribute of perseverance and endurance was imparted to me. It was perhaps the reason I continued to march toward a better future and the resolution of the health issues I would later develop.

In contrast, my father, who passed away about fifteen years ago, was firm in his spiritual convictions. He was a religious person, a follower and lover of his favorite Hindu goddess, Durga. Goddess Durga is known to be a warrior who knows how to fight and drive the demons out. Her devotees believe she possesses divine shakti (feminine force and energy) which she uses to combat evil and negative powers, as well as protects her followers from the forces of wickedness and misery.

8

Growing up, I watched Mom prepare special meals for Dad during his fasting time for Durga, but she never participated in these rituals. Having witnessed from a young age my aunts and grandmother engaging in religious activities and worshipping their gods, I used to think praying and fasting was for women and not for men. In our household, however, it worked conversely; Dad conducted the religious ceremonies and carried out Hindu traditions.

I loved the way Dad cleansed his temple, kept his idols in order, burned incense, and recited his devotions prior to going to work. To my surprise, he didn't have to read any of the Hindu slokas (scripture verses) or mantras (a set of sounds or words repeated in meditation) from any of his religious books because he had memorized them all. He used to talk about his spiritual journey of worshipping Durga since his teens.

I am grateful to my dad for planting a spiritual seed in me to pursue Hinduism at the age of ten. Through the years, I observed that he never wavered from his pious path or doubted his goddess Durga, despite the hardships he endured in his job, business, finances, and physical health. As a child, I followed in Dad's footsteps and developed the habit of chanting mantras and adoring the same goddess he exalted. I took the religious commitment personally and seriously. Like him, I tended to the idols at our home altar, cleansed them, dressed them in their proper attire, put flower garlands around them, lit a diya (oil lamp) before them as a form of worship, and left food on a plate in front of them as an offering. I would also visit neighborhood temples occasionally.

My childhood was beautiful. My sisters and I felt abundant love and affection from both parents while we grew up. A carefree and happy-go-lucky girl, I loved life and being myself. I was often complimented for being an amicable person. Overall, I was a sincere, hardworking, and studious child always striving for good grades. My parents stayed away from tradition here a bit, as our grades were not their priority, unlike most other Indian families. Their expectation of us was to work hard and accomplish what we could to the best of our abilities. They believed that if we persevered in our studies, it would bring us the desired results.

Having no pressure from parents brought balance and harmony into my life. I was able to engage in extracurricular activities, like badminton, cricket, track, and volleyball. It also left room for my own pursuit of spirituality. I would ponder questions: *Do we truly come back to life after our death according to the Hindu belief of reincarnation? How do we genuinely please gods and develop a closer relationship with them?* These thoughts fostered curiosity in me and made me look for answers in my little world, first as a child, then as an adult.

Both my parents' different perspectives about spiritual matters fascinated me. I observed Dad putting all his trust and confidence in Durga, whereas Mom sought out faith healers for solutions to overcome life's struggles. But the question which remained in my heart was: *Who should we trust and receive our blessings from: Hindu gods, faith healers, or both?*

Chapter 3

Who to trust, Gods or Faith Healers?

*I*n the Hindu religion, there is a trimurti (triune) god: Brahma, the creator; Vishnu, the preserver; and Shiva, the destroyer and regenerator of the universe. Under these three supreme gods, there are millions of representations of gods and goddesses. These various deities are incarnated, each in its own specific shape, size, and color. They each have their own significance and tasks in bringing universal order, blessings, and spirituality to those who worship them.

Idol worship is the way Hindus connect with their gods and goddesses. For decades, I followed this tradition faithfully, but at the same time, my heart wrestled with something. I was not fully convinced or content with the rigidity and religiousness of it; I somehow knew that there was more to it. The thought which I would often entertain was: *If god is a spirit with no form or shape, why is there a need to bow down and worship not one, but multiple gods and goddesses?*

There were moments when I'd look up at the blue sky from the veranda of our house and invite the supreme Hindu god to come in any feasible form he or she wished. I longed to have a

11

relationship and oneness with the highest Hindu god. There is a saying, *"Be careful what you wish for, as it might come true."* My wish did eventually come to pass, but it didn't come in a way that I ever could have imagined.

While growing up, I learned that Hindus believe in Karma (deed), a system of reward or punishment for one's actions, and Samsara (cycle of rebirth also known as reincarnation). They view pain and suffering from illnesses, poverty, premature death, hardships, incurable diseases, etc. in their current lives as the consequence of bad karma or evil deeds from their past lives. Subsequently, they also believe that the sinful actions of past lives can be worked out in their current lives by doing good deeds and earning merit for a better reincarnation. The goal for a Hindu is to be liberated from earthly desires and achieve Moksha (liberation) from the cycle of rebirth or reincarnation which comes after purification of one's soul and many births.

Hence, Hindus believe that a person's soul can be reborn with a better life by following any or all five religious practice steps in their current life: 1) Become a devotee to one or more deities from among the millions of Hindu gods and goddesses. The choice of deity being left up to the individual; 2) Continue to grow in religious knowledge through meditation, recitation of mantras and slokas, and reading scriptures; 3) Dedicate one's time to religious ceremonies, rituals, and rites; 4) Participate in fasting, prayers, and personal sacrifices; and 5) Visit holy places and/or go on pilgrimages.

Although Hinduism remains the prevalent religion throughout India, people also follow other religions including Christianity, Judaism, Islam, Sikhism, Jainism, Buddhism, and Zoroastrianism. Each of these faiths are unique in their belief systems and views of their God or gods. Indians, and Hindus in particular, are comfortable and interested in learning about others' religions, but most will not divorce themselves from their faith. It surprised me to learn, later in life, that I am one of the exceptions.

From my experience, I can tell that most people in India are warmhearted, welcoming, open minded, and tolerant of others' opinions, beliefs, cultures, and political views. This was the very reason my parents gave me freedom to initiate my spiritual quest by visiting gathering places of other religions like Sikh gurudwaras, Islamic mosques, Buddhist temple, and Jain temple. I could not locate a church or synagogue in the vicinity and therefore had no exposure to either Christianity or Judaism.

Faith healers, a prominent feature in Indian communities, were another option for me, as they were readily available on every street corner of Delhi. They primarily serve clients through their expert spiritual techniques and advice in astrology, palm and horoscope reading. My family – mostly my mom – like many other families in India, availed themselves of these services; and, of course, I was also exposed to this kind of spiritual system.

Of all the faith healing options, astrology is the most sought after. It is not uncommon for a Hindu parent to inquire from an astrologer about the blessings a newborn brings into his or her life. Answers to questions pertaining to different phases of one's life, such as the ideal time frame for marriage, financial and professional matters, health problems, even indicators leading to an untimely death can all be addressed via one's horoscope.

While growing up, I saw Mom being drawn into the allure of astrologers, and she would often receive predictions from them for her family members and their future. Soon after I was born, Mom had her astrologer create my horoscope scroll. She was eager to find out all the fine details of my life. Dad mostly stayed away from these "spiritual advisors," but occasionally he would give in to Mom's request and go along with her just to check them out.

As a teen, I recall an astrologer told me that India wouldn't be my permanent home, as I would settle down for good in a foreign land. Another one told me I would have a female hormone-related disease at some point in my life. When I remember these two predictions, I realize these did come to pass. On the other hand, their many other prophecies over my life turned out to be false.

Astrologers are not only notorious for forecasting our future but giving us remedies for the difficult phases of our lives. I remember one of the astrologers instructed me to wear a yellow topaz ring on my right index finger because of its wonderful health, academic, and professional benefits. In addition, I was told that the ring would also bring good luck, fame, success, and favor. I trusted his advice and wore the prescribed zodiac ring for a long time, but it didn't do what he promised it would. With time, I began to realize that the fortune-telling services were nothing more than an addiction to my soul, and a short-lived one, albeit a comforting spiritual pill for my pain and misery.

Another commonly used service in India is that of so-called spiritual doctors who carry what is believed to be magical insight to help uncover the cause behind their clients' personal and family problems. They use their spiritual powers to ward off evil spirits they believe may be the reason for wreaking havoc in one's life. During difficult times in our family, my parents contacted them and followed their counsel. In the end, their solutions brought no fruitful results.

What bothered me most was that if Hindu gods were there for us, why did we have a need to contact faith healers, astrologers, or spiritual doctors? The gods were supposed to take care of our needs and wish lists. I wholeheartedly believed each of the Hindu gods and goddesses was equipped to give us their divine solutions and shower us with their blessings and favor. In due time, they would have brought healing into every area of our lives.

Unfortunately, it did not happen that way, as my dad continued to go around the same mountain of worshipping and pleading his case to Durga in vain. It brought him more discouragement, hopelessness, and stagnation than he even realized, yet he patiently continued to do the same ritual he had learned and practiced throughout his life. At times, I wondered whether his prayers were heard in heaven. If they were, why would the gods, especially Durga, not have mercy upon my dad or bring him desirable results?

For a long time, I lived under the belief that Durga and other Hindu gods were extremely busy with their heavenly affairs; that was the reason the answer to our prayers had not come yet but would eventually. This convincing thought encouraged me to keep marching forward without making much ado about it, and perhaps it did the same for Dad too.

In hindsight, my parents believed we were in some kind of god-given test. Its purpose was to see if we would continue to stand firm in our faith regardless of our challenges or give in to our fears and give up on our gods. This left me in limbo. *Which should I lean on: faith or fear since both seemed real?*

15

Chapter 4

Faith versus Fear

*A*t the age of thirteen, personal health issues sprang up seemingly out of the blue. One of them was the sudden disappearance of my monthly cycle. I was shocked at first, then I pondered this change and turned to prayer: *What could be the reason for this sudden shift?* I hoped and prayed for my cycle to be restored in the coming months, but it did not.

All Mom said was, "Why don't you let go of your concerns for the time being and do not overanalyze your situation." I followed her advice for a while, but it hit me hard when my periods showed no signs of returning for another year. She then decided to take me to the best gynecologist in town and have me evaluated. The doctor had me go through many blood tests in the hopes of understanding and relieving the problem. Fortunately, my test results were normal, showing no abnormalities in female hormone levels. She instructed me to wait a little longer and assured me that my cycle would normalize. It was just a matter of time.

In the interim, I rested and waited for six months. I made a conscious effort not to fret but continue to stay optimistic. To my surprise, Mom was unable to stay calm. It did not take her long to make appointments with two more doctors, so she could get second and third opinions about this mysterious condition.

Upon our meeting with one of the gynecologists, the doctor discerned that polycystic ovarian syndrome (PCOS) could be the reason behind the missing cycles. With this evaluation came a recommendation for me to have an ovarian biopsy procedure. My parents and I gave serious thought to her advice, and in a couple of weeks, we opted to have it done. During the procedure, the doctor detected cysts on my ovaries and removed them through an incision in my abdomen. We rejoiced with positive thoughts that my menstrual problem was now a thing of the past. We gleefully anticipated no more delays; the periods would resume soon.

My hopes elevated, and I could hardly wait to see the positive outcome of the procedure. We were patient, yet expectant, during this testing time. Shockingly, six months went by again, and there were no signs of the return of my cycle. This reality was unbearable, as we knew there were no medical options left to overcome this hurdle. That's when I believed the symptoms must simply be part of my genetics and nothing else could be done.

The doctor's plan was to put me on prescribed hormone pills to help regulate my periods. She told me that this medical option would not cure the problem but superficially regularize my monthly cycle as long as I continued to ingest the pills. Although I felt devastated and shattered to hear that this was my only option, I had no other choice but to accept it. Even still, my inner voice did not let me stop at that. I felt there had to be a better answer. I became more intentional and pursued Durga at our home altar, day and night, for her divine intervention and resolution of these health issues.

During this intense time of prayer, I noticed the appearance of unwanted facial hair around my chin and face. I became conscious of my looks and would often compare it with my school friends. The more I scrutinized and analyzed my facial hair in the mirror, the more I felt depressed and ashamed. I had no idea how to get rid of it, but with time and experimentation, I learned how to use cosmetic bleach and was satisfied with the results.

Camouflaging my facial hair did provide some relief, but I was still plagued by negative thoughts about my unattractiveness. These depressing thoughts convinced me that I was destined to remain in this emotional pit for life. I longed to be set free from them, but I did not know how.

Even though I felt life didn't play fair, I was too young to give up. Mom continued to encourage me. As stated, she was a fighter by nature and did not quit easily. She was burdened to see me downtrodden about my health problems, and her heart was filled with sadness, yet she continued to fix her eyes on a solution. She became excited when one of her friends spoke highly of a Muslim healer and his healing powers. I thought we were done with mystics, but Mom convinced me to see this man who was highly recommended. I conceded, thinking I had nothing to lose.

Upon arrival at the healer's mosque, he first asked personal health-related questions and afterwards, invited Mom and I to his sanctuary. There, he had me drink a glass of what looked like milk, over which he recited healing prayers. He then asked me to lay down on a cement bed. As soon as I finished the mystery drink, I started to vomit. It was obvious he expected this reaction and explained that the drink cleansed my digestive and reproductive system and removed the "evil spirits"

19

which had been lodged inside me. He uttered more prayers and assured us that I was healed. We accepted his explanation and were grateful for my healing. We confidently stood by his conviction for the next few months. But nothing changed.

When problems are many and remedies are few, there is a human tendency to continue to look for answers in as many directions as it takes. Seeking healers was my mom's expression of faith. What happens to many people in India who are hooked on faith healing is that no matter how hard they pursue it, healing becomes a destination they can never reach. They succumb to a vicious cycle of hope and despair, moving from healer to healer, from one who 'failed' to another who will surely be more intuitive and effective.

Mom was disappointed that the Muslim healer did not cure me, but it certainly did not discourage her. She continued to search, and by word of mouth, she found another healing guru. His miracles at healing were impressive; she felt overly confident. Initially, she went alone to meet him and seek his counsel. Once convinced of his healing power, she scheduled an appointment for my deliverance session which was to be a month-long wait. The guru told her that he and his assistant would examine my physical situation and use their healing powers to bring wholeness into my body.

Mom wholeheartedly felt that under the blessings of *this healer*, I would be victorious and set free from my heartaches and ailments. Her positivity and strong conviction impressed me, and with renewed hope, I decided to go see him. At the healing session, I was told I would have to be alone with the guru and his assistant. Mom would be called in to speak with them toward the end. At sixteen years old, the idea of being myself under the influence of these strangers was scary to us.

Our fears were assuaged only a bit when Mom was allowed to stay right at the entrance of the room we were in and watch me from there.

With as much courage as I could muster, I stepped into their healing room. First, the three of us had a cordial conversation, and I was then asked to sit in front of them. Next, the guru put a lit tea light candle in his right palm and brought it closer to my face. While they both chanted prayers over me in a loud voice, the guru began to move his right palm in small arcs from the top of my head to feet. It only took them a few minutes to be done with their therapy. I noticed other clients were sitting outside waiting their turn. It was a busy day for the healers.

After the healing session, the guru assured us that their prayers had already brought wholeness and divine alignment into my body. There would be no follow-up, they explained, since they were confident that my body was already healed and restored. We waited patiently to see the results. But after a few months, their deliverance brought zero relief to my medical problems.

At this crossroad, I readied myself to bear the burden of my condition and decided not to pursue faith-healing as an alternative solution. I made up my mind that neither Mom nor anyone else could entice or persuade me to visit faith healers anymore. I thought of their healing power as hocus-pocus, rather than divine. I had seen enough.

The faith healing path tested and twisted my trust beyond limit. What I learned from this experience is that every spiritual door does not lead to the divine solution or truth. I saw how easy it was for me to make a mistake by either travelling down unknown spiritual paths or seeking help from unknown spiritual healers. The wide spiritual road could bring chaos, confusion, distraction, and destruction to my life without me even knowing it. As I let go of faith healing, I wondered: *Was there a way out of my misery, and if so, how and from where would my help come?*

Chapter 5

Depression

I was seventeen and a freshman in college, when yet another mysterious infirmity appeared. I had not yet found answers to the lack of my monthly cycle and unsightly facial hair; in addition, the hair on my scalp started to shed. Mom was the first one to notice and was alarmed to see how thin the hair had become. This drastic hair loss baffled me, as I'd never heard of such a strange symptom before. So, I began to monitor my hair closely every time I washed or combed it. I did my best to style it a certain way, so the balding spots wouldn't be noticeable, but it was impossible to hide.

Over time, I became obsessed with my hair loss. Every time I combed it, I found mounds of hair all over the floor and covering my clothes. I feared I would become bald and soon became distraught. Most teenagers want to look pretty. I certainly did, and now, at an age when self-confidence and physical beauty mattered most, I had unwanted facial hair *and* impending baldness.

When I finally roused myself to act, I decided to seek out a homeopathic doctor. I knew that a holistic approach aims at the root cause of disease, rather than simply alleviating its symptoms. Homeopathic medicine is different from conventional medicine, as it uses natural remedies to treat a patient's whole being, rather than focusing on a single diseased body part.

As a new patient, I underwent a detailed, comprehensive interview with the doctor. My responses gave her an understanding of my physical, psychological, and emotional state. Then, she prepared a homeopathic concoction pertaining specifically to my condition. The holistic medicine came in dry, pellet form, but the doctor diluted it in a solution customized to my medical history and needs. The pellets were tiny in size, easily dissolvable in the mouth, tasteless, and convenient to carry around.

Every other week, when I went to the homeopathic doctor for a prescription refill, the doctor would ask about my progress. Based on the input, she would adjust the medicine and its potency. I followed this inexpensive regimen faithfully for a year without any positive outcome.

Prior to and during the treatment, I was upbeat, as I had faith in this holistic cure. But after a year with no results and no resolution of the problem, I decided to discontinue the regimen. With no hope of a cure, my obsession and self-consciousness worsened. This helpless situation brought a new level of sadness to my heart that I didn't anticipate. I tried hard to shake the negativity off and focus on other things, but I just couldn't.

Next, I began to experience severe heaviness and fogginess in my head. Soon the initial symptoms developed into an ongoing, throbbing headache which would linger most of the day. The only time I found relief was when I slept at night, but the moment I would wake up, my headaches would return. Despite these difficulties, I continued to attend college but struggled to keep up with my studies.

Eventually, as days, weeks, and months passed, I could no longer handle depressive thoughts. That's when I decided to seek help from our family practitioner. I was diagnosed with clinical depression, and the doctor prescribed antidepressants to me. He said the medication would lift the gloom, as well as address severe headaches. At first, the drug seemed to alleviate symptoms, as it would numb the pain in my head for an extended period, and that alone lifted my spirits. However, the moment its effects wore off, I sank lower in depression.

At this juncture, I lost interest in everything, other than my family. Depression is notorious for sapping one's emotional strength and energy and keeping one locked in the vicious cycle of discouragement, hopelessness, and powerlessness. This was my situation, and I was desperate to be freed from its shackles. Despite its debilitating impact, depression didn't deter me from my quest to find an answer from either medicine or religion. I still had faith that one or the other would bring me relief from misery if I would just be patient. My faith at this point might not have been much more than a little glimmer, but it gave me enough determination to move forward.

More than anyone else, the chemist friend at the pharmacy seemed to understand my situation. Every time I went to his shop to get prescription refills, he shared his concerns with me. He was reluctant to continue filling my prescription; he felt I was too young to be dependent on antidepressants. To wean myself from the medication, he talked to me about its side effects and encouraged me to overcome headaches on my own. Although his uplifting words were powerful, they could not pull me out of my situation or dissuade me from continuing the medication. This sickness had total control over me.

I continued to take the antidepressants daily, as it helped numb the pain and relax my mind. However, as time went on, I realized the prescribed dosage was no longer enough for me. Within a couple of hours of me taking the pills, the severe headaches would return. Out of desperation, I took matters into my hands and increased the dosage by adding an extra pill to the prescribed amount. It helped me to an extent, but it didn't bring any lasting cure.

In hindsight, these events ate up eight years of my precious young life, from the age of seventeen until twenty-four. My depression started when I was a freshman in college and continued throughout the college years. Even when I took a full-time job immediately after graduation, the depression lingered. I managed the busy schedule of work and home, but it didn't help stop my depression or its symptoms.

As time went on, Mom's outlook changed. She no longer sought assistance or remedies from her faith healers for my ailments. Perhaps she finally realized that these healers were not effective. Like me, she might have felt helpless and struggled with these questions, the answers to which were elusive: *What should one do and where could we find the answers to problems such as missing monthly cycles, shedding hair, overgrowth of facial hair, and ongoing depression?*

Chapter 6

Coming to America

I felt stuck in my physical and emotional misery in India. My depression wasn't lifting, and I realized I needed something new. At this point, a desire that had been quelled, a desire that I had since I was a teen, somehow re-ignited itself. I dreamed of traveling to the United States of America for many years, and this yearning returned to me, despite the cloud of negativity I was in. *Why America, and not some other country?* I cannot explain the reason. It was like an inner sense that this was to be part of my destiny. I could no longer ignore or dismiss it. Now was the time.

At the age of twenty-four, I took a bold step to visit the U.S. Embassy of New Delhi and apply for a visa. I didn't seek any advice from my parents, nor did I rely on the services of the travel agencies in town. I simply showed up at the Embassy on my own. By then, I had heard stories from others that the U.S. ambassadors were notorious for rejecting visa applications, especially for youth in their twenties. I was anxious as to how it would work out for me. I knew that if the Embassy rejected one's visa application, the applicant must wait at least two years before reapplying.

Upon arriving at the Embassy, I waited patiently in the waiting room until my name was called to have a brief interview with the assigned U.S. ambassador. I had no idea until the very end of my interview whether I would be given a U.S. visa or not. To my great surprise, the officer stamped my passport with the U.S. visa and congratulated me. My dream to touch American soil was beginning to come true.

Since my parents had heard my heartfelt desire to travel to the U.S. for so many years, they had no objections when I asked their permission to go. Dad was a bit hesitant about me going alone, so he decided to contact an Indian family who he knew in Houston, Texas. To our delight, Dad's friends agreed to receive and accommodate me for the initial stay there. Their gracious offer of hospitality not only made me feel comfortable leaving India, but it also eased Dad's concern and gave him confidence that everything would go well for me in the U.S.

Finally, when the big day came, I bid my family goodbye and embarked on the overseas journey. It was a twenty-four-hour flight from New Delhi to Houston with a stop in Amsterdam. By the time the plane landed in Houston, I was tired and jet lagged but anxious to meet this new family. Much to my relief, the Chopras were waiting for me at the terminal. Mrs. Chopra was there along with her mother-in-law and nephew. Although they did not have a sign with my name on it, our intuition helped us connect with each other easily. Soon after our meeting, it became clear that they were friendly and warm-hearted folks. I could easily talk with the Chopra family in English and Hindi. I also felt comfortable in their company, so I knew I was in safe hands.

Their residence was quite a distance from the airport which gave me a chance to peek at the city of Houston and get a feel for the area. It appeared to be flat and was surrounded by buildings of various shapes and sizes, just like New Delhi. The roads were wider and cleaner, and the highways were much broader than back home. The city was well lit in the evening, and it looked inviting and charming. Although I was excited to be in this new place which reminded me of my hometown, I was nervous about the unknowns ahead.

Despite my quick friendship with the Chopra family, I missed my family back home. Initially, it was hard for me to be alone in a foreign land, as I had never been away from home until then. I could only call home every other month, as it was prohibitively expensive. Mostly, I would interact with my family members via letters through the U.S. mail, as there was no email or texting in those days. It was not easy to start a brand-new life and adjust to Western culture, but I knew in my heart I had come to America for a reason. What that reason was I did not yet know.

After a week of living with the Chopras, I moved into my own place – a tiny, inexpensive, one bedroom apartment near them. Their nephew lived in the same apartment complex, and he helped me get my bearings initially by taking me to grocery stores, the post office, and other places in town when I asked. It took me a year to overcome homesickness, make friends, get to know the city and its public transportation system, learn to cook food, and so on.

Greater Houston reminded me of New Delhi in numerous ways. It is the fourth largest city in the United States and is home to a large Indian population. As I explored the city, I found all that I needed: Indian grocery stores, Bollywood music on cassettes and movies on video tapes, traditional Indian clothes and jewelry, and even inexpensive air travel to

India. In addition, there are several Hindu temples, North and South Indian restaurants, and social gathering places for the Indian community. As I grew familiar with my new surroundings, I no longer missed Delhi since Houston had it all. This made my decision to stay in the U.S. easier.

Despite adapting to my new life and environment, I found myself still struggling with depression and the other symptoms I had before. It seemed that the old baggage followed me from India to America. Depression was still a part of my life. Hence, I had no choice but to live with it. I chose not to depend upon medication anymore, as the antidepressants I took in India did not permanently relieve the symptoms. I continued to experience severe headaches, which lasted sometimes for weeks and other times for months with little reprieve in between. Now, I had no one to share my concerns with and no one to comfort me. The phone conversations with my parents were few and far between.

Initially, my life was lonely; but, with time, I was able to make friends with a couple of Indian women. One of them became my bosom buddy, as we connected on a deeper level emotionally right from the start. Bindu went out of her way to be there for me when I needed her. She was a selfless and compassionate woman who became like an older sister to me. I thank God for making us cross paths and for bonding us together. *How rare it is to find such a precious friend!*

Over time, our friendship grew stronger, and we developed a special bond. Bindu would come and visit me as often as she could with her two-year old daughter. She loved the different kinds of Indian breads I would make for her. We went shopping together and occasionally ate out at restaurants. This kind of intimate sisterly relationship helped join our hearts together, as we began to share our inner thoughts and feelings. I would be there to listen and comfort her when she shared her heartaches and challenges in life, and she did the same for me. We valued each other's' companionship.

After I became more comfortable in her company, I started to pour out my heart to her and felt free discussing my struggle with depression. She was a patient soul who stood by me during my darkest days, and somehow helped me wrestle with my inner turmoil, as I struggled to find peace. With her comfort and encouragement, I began to cope with my depression in healthier ways. It felt like Bindu was on a mission to bring me out of the dark valley.

Bindu's positive and upbeat influence lifted me from my depression slowly but surely. My headaches became bearable and less severe than before; their duration shortened, and their frequency lessened. I started to feel much lighter as well as more free, mentally and emotionally. I could think with much more clarity since my mind wasn't clouded with acute headaches. What a difference my friend was making in my life!

Soon, I was on top of the world; I hadn't felt this wonderful in almost ten years. I never thought I would come out of depression. It was as though I was released from something. *My second miracle, after my first one as a survivor from a near-death accident!* It felt like Bindu somehow had authority over depression and an ability that neither medical doctors nor faith healers had. *But what was the quality that only she possessed?* I wasn't to find out until over a decade later.

I thanked the Hindu gods for sending Bindu into my life and answering long-awaited prayers to overcome the throbbing headaches and depression. It was a turning point which helped me become more optimistic than ever before. This second miracle made me look at the brighter side of life and no longer doubt the gods' divine powers.

Right from the start, when Bindu and I connected, it became apparent that there was something subtly powerful about her that I could not figure out. It was unsettling in a way, but I made a conscious decision to bury my curiosity and didn't think about it much. In almost every conversation she and I had, she'd mention God and his characteristics. At the time, I didn't understand which god she was talking about, but I felt assured that Bindu's god could bring me out of my doldrums. I did not ask any questions, nor did I show any interest in her spirituality. I simply continued to allow her profound influence to flow into me.

Bindu never used any name for her god; she simply called him "God." Like me, she was raised Hindu and migrated from India to the U.S. I casually thought she must be referring to one of the many Hindu gods. Perhaps asking her about which god she was referring to might have violated her privacy, or sabotaged our friendship, which I would never want to do with someone who I cherished so dearly. I had found a treasure in her comforting and soothing nature.

We seemed to be in sync with each other's heartbeat; she could read my thoughts before I would utter them. As an empathetic person, Bindu felt my emotions exactly as I experienced them. It went beyond mere kindness and tenderheartedness. She cried as I cried when I felt pain. When I needed consoling, she was stern, and her honesty would cut through me until I could see the truth. Bindu possessed caring qualities and wisdom which seemed to come naturally to her. Like a sponge, I absorbed her suggestions and advice, as she poured them into me.

Sometimes my curiosity would surface, and I would wonder, *could it be her inner makeup that made her who she was ~ calm, kind, patient, compassionate, loving, and selfless? Or was it the god that she worshipped? How did she have such peace and joy in her heart, and how could she convey it so easily to another person?* Either knowingly or unknowingly, Bindu was depositing a hunger in me to search for eternal meaning which I'd always longed for.

My friend understood something which I didn't at the time, that everything on earth happened at its appointed time. She might not have mentioned her god's name specifically because she might have felt it would be better to wait and see how things would unfold for me. My curiosity was beginning to rise to the surface more and more frequently; but still, even after years, I chose not to delve deeper and probe her about her beliefs. I was still young and carefree, probably not ready to pursue the path she was on.

While my relationship with Bindu continued to grow, I was introduced to an older Indian couple, the Singhs, in Houston through a mutual friend of ours. Upon speaking with them over the phone, they invited me to their Presbyterian church on the following Sunday morning. I was curious: *Why church and not their house or a restaurant for us to meet?*

Chapter 7

My Church Invitation

I had never attended a Christian church service before, so visiting one felt awkward. I did not know what to expect or how the congregation would react to me. Despite my anxiety, I pushed through and honored the Singhs' request to meet them at the Presbyterian church. When I arrived, they welcomed me with warm hugs and invited me to sit with them. Although we did not have a chance to speak before the service began, I knew in my heart that I was at the right place, at the right time, and with the right people. Looking back, I believe it was a divine appointment.

Their church was small, and the people were friendly. I enjoyed the pastor's simple and upbeat message about his God, Jesus. After his sermon, the congregation recited "The Lord's Prayer" then sang the verse from *Joshua 24:15, "As far as me and my house, we will serve the Lord; we will serve the Lord."* The church service concluded with everyone partaking in the Communion of the Lord, so I followed their tradition of taking a piece of bread and juice after their pastor prayed over it. When the service ended, the Singhs took me to a Chinese restaurant for lunch. In the relaxing atmosphere of the restaurant, we were able to sit comfortably and get to know each other better. They were a gracious and wonderful couple. I felt loved and appreciated in their company.

The following week was undoubtedly the most peaceful week I had ever experienced. The ailments I had been contending with still lingered, but for the first time, I felt an extraordinary joy in my heart and a stillness in my mind. As the week progressed, I enjoyed this "new me," while I continued the daily routine of idol worship at my apartment altar. I thought: *What was so special about the church service that brought such positivity and calmness in my soul?* I pondered this new feeling all week long.

This feeling was so consuming that I wanted to experience it once again. I chose to go back to the church the following Sunday, since I had no problem worshipping Jesus and the Hindu gods at the same time. Soon, I was attending church service every Sunday as it gave me purpose, hope, and, with each visit, a sense of optimism.

Gradually, I began to develop a strong bond with the Singhs. Not only were they loving and compassionate; they treated me like their daughter and took me under their protective wings, like parents. They rescued me when my car was in trouble, and they comforted me when I felt lonely and homesick. They also gave me an open invitation to visit them any time. I knew they were a blessing, just as Bindu was, but I was to learn later just how important a gift they were. I became so comfortable with them; I found myself sharing my work, personal, and financial challenges. In return, I received encouragement and sound advice on how to go about tackling and overcoming them. I began thinking of them as my extended family. I am forever grateful to the Singhs for not only showering me with their unconditional love but introducing me to Jesus and His church.

Despite the beautiful experience the church gave me, I still saw Jesus as a foreign god - the God of Christianity. I could not differentiate spiritually between Jesus and Hindu gods, as my understanding of Christianity as a religion and its teachings were limited only to Sunday services. But one thing I knew for sure was that visiting Hindu temples did not give me the same tangible feeling of God's presence that I got in church.

I contemplated more deliberately as time went on, *what differentiated Hinduism from Christianity?* I received no answers, but I continued to feel drawn to Sunday services at church. As much as I loved attending the services, I started fearing that my gods would be upset with me if I followed Jesus. My way of getting around this internal conflict was to continue my idol worship at home every day except Sundays when I looked forward to the pastor's sermon.

Even though I enjoyed everything about this Christian church, I knew I would never step out of the Hindu religion or offend the gods and goddesses. Never. That would be a disgrace to my immediate and extended family and an insult to the gods. But Jesus had a different plan for me.

Chapter 8

Long Awaited
Prayers Answered

*C*hurch, and all the joy it brought, gave me a bright and promising outlook on life. However, my personal life still had challenges. Days were long at work where I struggled to develop meaningful relationships with co-workers. Every evening, when I returned to my apartment, there was no one to talk to and share my concerns with. Watching television diverted my attention a bit from a stressful day at work, but it didn't help alleviate any of my inner emotional turmoil.

One of my biggest challenges was dealing with my immediate supervisor, Bob. Rather than gaining a growing sense of self-esteem and confidence at work, I felt beaten down. Bob was critical of me and the quality of my performance. It seemed he would find fault just with me, not with the other employees. I didn't quite understand his behavior, but I never questioned him or his authority. I tried to mind my own business and stay out of his way. I remained with this job only because I needed the salary.

Another challenge was finding the right man so I could spend quality time getting to know him and eventually get married. I tried meeting young men through Indian organizations and friends, but these avenues did not work for me. As difficult as it was to find a suitable man, I didn't give up hope. However, I questioned my Hindu god, Shiva, when my prayers to be married went unanswered.

Shiva is the favorite god of almost every young Hindu woman who seeks him to receive his marital blessings for an ideal life partner. Since my teenage days, I had worshipped Shiva, performed rituals, and fasted on Mondays to please him. However, I didn't have any luck in meeting a decent man in Houston, despite it having a large Indian population. I blamed myself for my continued singleness. I believed that if only I had fasted and worshipped Shiva enough, I would have found a suitable match.

Little did I know that going to church, worshipping Jesus, and taking prayers to Him every Sunday service would have a positive and rewarding impact on my life. Soon, I was able to find a better job opportunity in another department of the same company. My new boss was not only a kind person, but he appreciated my work and treated me with respect. I believe it was another divine intervention of Jesus, but I did not understand that at the time. I called it luck or a fluke when things worked out in my favor and instead, thanked the gods for their blessings.

Another prayer was answered when Shobu Mukerjee arrived in Houston from North Carolina for a job-related conference. The Singhs knew Shobu's parents from many years before when they lived in Houston, and this man was precious to them. They wanted us to meet, and after hearing about each other, we both agreed. I decided to extend an invitation. On the day of his arrival, after he checked into his hotel, I took

Shobu to a famous four-story mall called Galleria. There, we enjoyed window shopping a bit and watching people skate on an ice-rink. Later, we went to a restaurant for dinner and as we talked, his levelheaded, down to earth, and kind-hearted nature captured my interest.

Shobu and I bonded well as friends during his brief visit in Houston. Before he departed, we exchanged contact information, but I felt it was more out of courtesy than anything else. I had no plans to move forward with him due to my apprehension about a long-distance relationship, but God had a different plan for both of us.

When Shobu called me a week later, I was delighted, and my concerns about the distance between us disappeared. From then on, we continued to stay in touch over the phone, and our friendship grew deeper. After a few months, he invited me to visit his parents during Christmas break in Cincinnati where they lived. I gladly accepted his invitation. His parents welcomed me lovingly and warmly and made my stay at their house comfortable. The more we got to know one another, the more I fell in love with Shobu and his parents. Upon my return to Houston, we continued our courtship over the phone, and a couple of months later, he asked to visit me again in Houston. I was delighted and looked forward to spending more time together.

On this visit, Shobu gave me the surprise of my life when he asked for my hand in marriage. First, he gave me a beautiful bracelet and helped me put it on my wrist. When he saw my joyful reaction to the bracelet, he took a ring out of his pocket and proposed to me. I will always treasure that breathtaking moment. I couldn't have been happier or felt more honored to accept his proposal. I knew in my heart that he was the one with whom I wanted to spend the rest of my life. It did not take us long to start thinking about our next steps for the wedding. Looking back, I know it was Jesus' plan all along, as everything we planned fell into place effortlessly.

We delayed the wedding until my parents could come from India, so they could meet Shobu and be with us on our wedding day. We had a civil wedding, and I only invited close friends including Bindu and her family. Unfortunately, Bindu could not attend, as she now lived in California, but she rejoiced and celebrated with me over the phone. Our wedding reception was a joyous occasion, as there was a great sense of love and connection between everyone there. We postponed our honeymoon for a later date, as my parents had only a few more days left to spend with us before their return to India.

I realize now that it was Jesus who blessed me with my wonderful husband and his family, in addition to a surprise gift. I had won an all-expense paid, seven-day cruise for two to Cozumel, Cancun, and Jamaica when my name was drawn at the office Christmas party. It was the perfect present at the perfect time. A honeymoon trip! Since I had never won anything in my life, I was surprised and beyond excited to receive this blessing. *Was this a beautiful gift from Jesus, were my Hindu gods finally responding to my prayers, or was it just dumb luck?*

With Shobu having a decent job in North Carolina, it made perfect sense for me to leave Houston and relocate to his hometown. I didn't move immediately after our wedding, but there was a period of three months from the time of our marriage to my relocation. During the last days in Houston, I continued to stay in touch with the Singhs. I called Bindu frequently, and we talked for hours on end. I also loved spending time with my Indian friends on the weekends. I knew I would probably not see them again. It was a bittersweet moment to let go of close contacts.

I was completely unaware at the time that I would also be leaving behind my one – and – most precious friend, Jesus. I was not sure if I wanted to accept Jesus as my God, but I enjoyed visiting His church for personal reasons. I still felt an internal happiness and peace every time I visited the church. I did not find this kind of tranquility at my apartment altar or at temples in Houston or Delhi.

Despite evidence of Jesus' power and presence in my life, my relationship with Him was just a Sunday event. Even when I felt His tangible presence at church, I didn't make much ado about it. I continued to wrestle with differentiating between the Hindu gods and Jesus. Although I praised my gods for the divine favor I received each time, I could not ignore the positive changes that were happening due to my visits to church. A quiet little voice kept telling me that it was Jesus who bestowed His blessings upon me and helped me overcome hurdles. But I ignored the whispers and held onto Hinduism.

Outwardly, I continued to prepare for a new life with Shobu, but inwardly I wrestled with the question of which spiritual path to take. Sometimes I credited Jesus with my answered prayers; other times I praised the Hindu gods for bringing me luck. But deep down, I knew that ever since I started going to church, God's blessings were chasing me down. I couldn't deny that Jesus' peace, which I felt during the church services, stayed with me throughout the following week. Also, the emotional and mental heaviness I carried for years was so much lighter than before. I was at ease and not worried as much about my struggles.

However, the uneasiness remained and the lack of spiritual clarity in my mind overshadowed my heart. I continued to struggle with indecisiveness about choosing and committing to a religious path. Perhaps, this pull between my heart and mind, and the confusion it caused, kept me from stepping out of my comfort zone of idol worship. I understood I had to forsake one path to follow the other, but I was stuck. I didn't truly know Jesus at this point, and that made it even more difficult to move forward in His direction and accept Him as my God. Sticking to my generational roots made perfect sense to me, and that's where I chose to stay. Of course, I took the easy way out and concluded: *If it was meant for me to be Jesus' disciple in the future, it would happen at His will and appointed time.*

I meekly told Shobu about my visits to the church on Sundays, and how its services made me feel. He had no reaction or response. Perhaps my apprehension and fear about following both religions at the same time got in the way of bringing it to my husband's attention more boldly and having a serious, open discussion about it. I was not sure how he might have reacted if I had explained how profoundly it affected me. I didn't bring it up again but continued to think about it. *Would I ever be able to attend a church service in North Carolina? Would Shobu allow me to pursue Hindu gods and Jesus at the same time?* These questions would remain unanswered for the next fourteen years.

Chapter 9
A New Life Without Church

*T*he wait to relocate was over! Shobu flew to Houston to help me pack up all my belongings. During his stay, the Singhs and other friends invited us for lunch and dinner at their houses, so we could spend some time together before we left. We both enjoyed their company and conversation dearly. On our day of departure, we loaded what we could in my car, including the Hindu altar, to take to our home in North Carolina.

I was excited to start a new chapter of life with my beloved. This was truly a dream come true! I looked forward to embracing what the future held for both of us in the coming months and years. My heart couldn't have been happier, and since I was able to dismiss my spiritual struggles amidst the flurry of excitement, my mind was finally at rest.

Now that I was settled in North Carolina, my priorities were clear: adjust to this new phase of life, find a job, and meet new friends. The thought of looking for a church and connecting with a new church family couldn't have been further from my mind. Inviting Jesus back into my life was not a desire anymore, as I was on cloud nine and happily married. Following gods within the parameters of Hinduism alone fit my life perfectly.

Within a couple of months of relocating, I was able to find the one and only one Hindu temple in the vicinity. I was excited to find that it had all the things I was looking for: the statues of several gods, including my favorite goddess, Durga, a Hindu priest and priestess, and a sanctuary where Hindus could get together and partake in the major Indian festivals, social events, and cultural programs. I felt right at home connecting once more to the Indian roots and traditions at the temple, and I yearned to be part of the congregation.

Almost all Hindus have either a big altar displaying multiple idols or a small altar keeping a couple of their favorite gods at their home. They don't mind having an idol or two in their place of work and many keep a mini-size idol on the dashboard of their cars. Having some god's symbol or picture gives them security and comfort in times of need and a feeling of godly protection from dangers and accidents. Sometimes, Hindus invite a temple priest to their new home or new business to bless their property and ward off evil spirits.

In the Hindu religion, if a husband worships his set of gods and a wife worships her set of gods, the couple doesn't mind worshipping each other's gods. Such was our case. Since we were both Hindus, I assumed Shobu would be keeping up with the Hindu traditions and rituals like most Hindu men. But he didn't bother acknowledging, worshipping, or bowing his head to any of the gods we had at our home altar. It was a bit strange for me to see this, but it didn't bother me. Growing up, I watched my dad take the spiritual lead in his marriage, so I thought maybe it was my turn to reciprocate in the same way in our marriage. I concluded that one partner in any given marriage tends to be more spiritual than the other, and that was fine with me.

As life went on, the Hindu temple in our town became my sanctuary for the Hindu deities. I would visit the temple whenever it held religious festivals. I would also make time on a regular basis to be part of the temple gatherings, and Shobu would tag along reluctantly with me. We met many Indian friends at the temple and before we knew it, our social circle grew and kept us busier than ever.

For the first four years, I felt blessed in every aspect of our married life. However, we knew it was time for us to start a family, especially since we had some pregnant friends and some with newborns. It felt like we were kind of left behind in a race of becoming parents. Shobu knew about my situation of not having periods, but it didn't seem to bother or stress him at all. Rather, he was upbeat and positive that we, as a couple, would beat the odds by getting medical help which would help us conceive without any trouble. His optimistic attitude brought joy to my heart and put me at ease. Although I did worry a bit, *what if this didn't work out the way we thought it would? Where would we then go to get help?*

Chapter 10

Uncertainties and Unknown Future

*A*fter a year of trying to conceive naturally with no results, we remained hopeful. Our inability to conceive wasn't shocking. Years earlier when doctors in India and the U.S. put me on the prescribed hormone pills to regulate my periods, they told me that I would need medical intervention to conceive. After we had done everything, we prepared ourselves mentally, emotionally, and physically to go through fertility treatment and stick with it, no matter the time and effort it might take for us to attain our goal.

Upon consulting with one of the OB/GYN (Obstetrician-Gynecologist) doctors in town, we were able to address our concerns. After reviewing my medical history and administering several tests, the doctor recommended that I go on fertility medication for conception. Shobu and I both agreed, and sure enough, it took only a month to see the fruitful results of my treatment. We were thrilled to be pregnant with our yet-to-be-born twins, a boy and a girl!

My pregnancy went smoothly until the end of the fifteenth week. One afternoon, while out to lunch with my co-workers, I felt a sudden, discomforting pain in my stomach. I had no idea what was wrong; I thought it might be the food that didn't agree with me. The pain stopped after a few minutes, so I dismissed it, but it returned in the middle of that night. First, I had a few minutes of pain, then there was a sudden gush of water when I sat on the toilet. Worried and scared, we immediately rushed to the emergency room. We were anxious while the doctors examined me, and waited with even more apprehension, as they tried to determine the cause. After further examination, the doctors told us that our son's gestational sac had ruptured, causing the leakage of amniotic fluid. They advised me to take a couple of weeks off from work and rest to see if the sac might seal itself. Sure enough, when I relaxed the next two weeks at home, I didn't experience any more episodes of leakage or discomfort.

During our next visit to the doctor, the OB/GYN physician repeated the ultrasound to see the condition of our son's gestational sac, and how he was responding to the trauma he went through. To our surprise and relief, she shared the good news that our son's sac somehow sealed itself, but the amniotic fluid around him was much less than normal. She decided to keep a close eye on my pregnancy and have me come in for checkups every other week. My pregnancy was at high risk since I was carrying twins, and the risk was even higher because the rupture in the gestational sac left our son vulnerable to infection.

Our twins and I did well until the twenty-fifth week. Then the telltale sign of water leakage let me know that our son's sac had a tear in it again. Shobu and I rushed to the hospital thinking I would deliver our babies. I was admitted to the hospital, and the team of OB/GYN doctors on call at the emergency room monitored me frequently throughout the night. The next morning, their collective decision was not to send me home, but rather keep me in the hospital until I was ready to deliver our twins.

I was in the hospital for two weeks when our son's sac ruptured a third time during the twenty-seventh week of pregnancy. I was taken immediately to the delivery room. The doctors believed I was ready to deliver, and it did not take me more than a few minutes to give birth to our twins that morning. I remember seeing both briefly after their birth and thinking how tiny they were. Our son was badly bruised due to the inadequate amount of fluid surrounding him in utero, but doctors told us this was a minor concern. Our daughter, however, looked perfect, despite her premature condition.

After waiting a couple of hours until the obstetrician and his team were finished examining our babies, the lead doctor came to tell us the good news: our son and daughter were in good health and responding well to the medical care they were getting! They assured us once again that the bruises on our son would fade in time, but their premature birth weight remained a concern, as they each weighed less than two pounds. The infants were immediately taken to the NICU (Neonatal Intensive Care Unit) where they had to stay in their individual incubators and were monitored closely. We were told that they would be released from the hospital only after they weighed at least five pounds. Although we were concerned about their prematurity, we chose to rejoice and celebrate their birth not knowing that sorrow was just around the corner.

In the early morning hours of the following day, one of the NICU nurses came in to tell us that our son was no longer alive;

his premature lungs could no longer sustain him. Shobu and I were shocked at first, since we had been blissfully imagining life with our two children. We were asked to say our final good-byes to him in the NICU. We took turns holding our son in our arms for a long time, and we cried uncontrollably. It was an emotional and heart-breaking day, the darkest day of our lives.

Within the next day or two, I was released from the hospital. Our daughter, who we named Anita, had to stay in the NICU until she weighed at least five pounds, could breathe on her own, and could eat without a tube. Once again, I took my sorrows to the Hindu gods at our home altar and asked them their reason for not saving our son. I heard nothing in response. I pleaded with them that they bestow their blessings upon our daughter while she was in NICU. Again, with no affirmation from the gods, I assumed they would divinely take care of her.

During her three-months stay in the NICU, I visited Anita every day. The nurses on duty encouraged me to put her on my chest and called it the "kangaroo" approach. This way, she could hear my heartbeat, as she did in the womb. Shobu visited too. After this three-month separation, and having reached many milestones, the doctors gave their approval for us to take our daughter home. Anita now weighed five pounds, two ounces.

Like all new parents, our lives were never to be the same after we brought our baby home. We had to take her to the pediatrician every two weeks, so she could monitor and check Anita's overall growth and development and give her the shots she needed. Her doctor made sure that she continued to thrive, breathed well on her own, reached the appropriate weight and height expectancies, and had good coordination. Anita's pediatrician was amazed at the progress she made in a short time. Upon receiving this good news, I gave credit and thanks to the Hindu gods for our daughter's development. We learned early on that Anita is another warrior from my side of the family, as she fought hard through every challenge and came out victoriously.

By the time Anita turned two, Shobu and I desired to have a second child. Of course, we knew my problem hadn't disappeared, and we would need help to conceive again. We accepted this, and after much discussion, we made an appointment with the OB/GYN. As expected, we were told I first had to go through a series of blood tests prior to my fertility treatment. But when the nurse called me the next day at work and gave my blood work report, I was stunned to hear what she had to say. I couldn't believe her at first, so I asked her to repeat it. She told me I was pregnant! This time, conception happened naturally. Shobu and I were ecstatic to hear this unbelievably good news. My pregnancy went smoothly for the entire nine months. I gave birth to our second daughter, Mia, right on her due date, and there were absolutely no complications during the delivery.

After the birth of our second daughter, my time centered around raising our two daughters, catering to their increasing needs, and handling a full-time job. It got to the point where my husband and I could no longer keep up with the hectic social lifestyle we developed over time. We also decided to cut back on our family visits to the temple.

During these busy years, the phone calls between Bindu and I also lessened. Being out of state and with a three-hour time difference between the East and West coasts, it became even more difficult to stay in touch with each other. Our communication, and the opportunities for us to meet, became less and less frequent. As time went by, the phone number I had always used for Bindu no longer worked. Occasionally, I would think of her and our treasured time together, but these memories faded with time. It felt like this was as far as our relationship was meant to go.

Despite a hectic schedule, there were times I found myself restless and uneasy. I tried hard to fill this void by putting more time and wholehearted efforts into worshipping and praising Hindu gods, but I came away feeling just as empty. My heart was still dissatisfied. I tried to go deeper and search for the reason behind this nagging and disturbing feeling, but I couldn't get closer to understanding it. Finally, I brushed off this feeling and attributed it to just a passing phase. I was sure I would bounce back to my normal self and that's exactly what happened. The desire to find answers eventually subsided, and I was able to move on.

By now, our daughters were about five years and two years in age, and they were both growing taller in stature and maturing in skills. I chose not to work and instead became a stay-at-home mom. I made a few friends through my daughters' play dates, but these friendships didn't give me the same kind of closeness I experienced with Bindu. She and I had enjoyed a special bond, an intimate companionship. My mind still returned to her from time to time and settled on a thought: *If it was meant for Bindu and I to reconnect, then whatever fate had connected us initially would make a way for us once again.*

Chapter 11

My Culprit Was Finally Revealed

*R*ight around the time our older daughter was in second grade and younger one was in preschool, I noticed two black spots, the size of an orange, appear in the center of my back. I didn't have any rash or irritation, so I couldn't imagine how, why, or when they appeared. It worried me, so I immediately made an appointment with a dermatologist. After he examined me, the doctor took a biopsy of each spot to evaluate whether they were benign or malignant. Fortunately, the biopsy report showed no signs of cancer, so it was good news...*but what were these black spots, and what made them suddenly appear?*

The dermatologist prescribed skin-fading cream for me to apply over the spots, assuring that they would fade away with time. After using the ointment for about six months, the black spots stayed just as they were, as dark as ever. Then another big black spot appeared on my lower right leg. The only difference was that this one was prominent; anyone could see it, depending on what I was wearing, and I was self-conscious about it. I tried different fading creams – the ones available over the counter and the one prescribed by my dermatologist – but neither had any effect on them.

One day, our younger daughter noticed a mass of lighter shades of black; this time they were more like patches blending into one another and covering my face like a mask. When I looked in the mirror and saw what she was talking about, I became alarmed. Each time I walked by a mirror, I began to check my face, and sure enough, the more I scrutinized it, the uglier I felt. Although I never tried to cover patches with makeup or foundation, the self-consciousness I felt as a teen suddenly returned; I was embarrassed for people to see my face. I wondered if it could be a blood disorder or hormonal changes causing this hyperpigmentation. *Were these dark spots to appear in more places?*

I made an appointment with my primary care physician, hoping she could assuage my worries, or better yet, cure me. She had no explanation as to the reason for my symptoms but expected to find out via lab results. The report revealed my hormone levels were normal except for the thyroid which was way off the range leaning toward hypothyroidism. She explained that signs and symptoms of hypothyroidism might vary from patient to patient, but most common symptoms included feeling fatigue, thinning hair, depression, weight gain, sensitivity to cold, muscle pain, irregular or lack of periods, infertility, and an enlarged thyroid gland, known as a goiter. This scared me.

Four of those symptoms jumped out at me. It felt like someone had turned a neon light bulb on in my head. A thyroid problem. As simple as that. All those years of worrying and suffering – the anxiety and shame I went through, the mysteries of sudden hair loss, lack of periods, clinical depression, and infertility – they had all been pointing to a deficiency in my thyroid gland! I was astonished to learn this, and I accepted the diagnosis right away. Finally, someone had found the culprit and I was grateful. The empirical evidence from a simple blood test had revealed the elusive puzzle piece at long last. This made me question the very history I lived through: *How did this diagnosis escape all the medical help I sought over the years?*

For the physician to treat my hypothyroidism, she told me I would have to be on Synthroid pills for the rest of my life. Shobu was not in favor of me taking this or any medication knowing that all pills have negative side effects. Together, we decided to postpone the idea of moving forward with the medication and waited to seek his dad's insight. His dad is a health scientist, and his advice was to take a supplement called "sea kelp" for at least three months to see its impact on my thyroid. He explained that iodine deficiencies are known to cause hypothyroidism and goiter formation. Sea kelp supports and helps stimulate the thyroid hormone, and it has been used for many years as a remedy for this problem. I decided to follow his suggestion.

After being on this supplement for a while, I went back to the primary care doctor and requested that she run another panel of tests on my thyroid. She agreed and immediately sent me to her lab, where they drew blood to check my TSH (Thyroid Stimulating Hormone), T3 (Triiodothyronine), and T4 (Thyroxine) levels. This time, my thyroid level numbers were lower than they were previously. When I told her about my sea kelp intake and my reasons for not taking the thyroid medication, she immediately referred me to the endocrinologist's care who was highly regarded in his field.

My father-in-law suggested I continue to follow the path he had put me on until the endocrinologist would instruct me otherwise. Upon meeting with this specialist for the first time, I told him about my supplement intake, and how it helped bring my thyroid levels down. He wanted to run additional lab tests as a baseline, so he could determine the best course of treatment for me. I was told to continue taking sea kelp until I met with him again after a couple of weeks for a follow-up.

At the follow-up visit, the thyroid levels were even better than before; the sea kelp was working and taking care of my thyroid deficiency. The endocrinologist encouraged me to continue taking the sea kelp, as there was no need to take any thyroid medicine. He also suggested that I see him once every six months, so he could track my progress and thyroid levels. Shobu loved his decision, and we were both relieved that I wouldn't have to be on any medication. Even with this good news, I had a nagging question in the back of my mind: *Would the sea kelp supplement work for life, or would it only give a temporary fix? If so, would I end up being on Synthroid later?* This question remained an unsolved mystery for ten more years.

Chapter 12

Downward Spiral of My Life

*W*ithin a couple of years of being diagnosed with hypothyroidism, my next symptom emerged out of nowhere and took me by complete surprise. I began to experience a mild pain in my lower back off and on, so I initially ignored it, thinking it was nothing but a temporary ache. I was confident it would go away on its own, and that I'd feel better within a day or two. Unfortunately, it didn't happen that way.

The pain was subtle in the beginning stages, but within a year, it became unbearable and excruciating. My upper body was fine, but the lower area had a constant pain, which would travel from my waist down to the legs and feet and come back up to the waist. This vicious cycle would continue throughout the day. I had no other choice but to consult my Internal Medicine doctor who, upon examination, prescribed painkillers to help ease this strange pain. She also sent me for X-rays of my lower body, but the results were normal.

While I was still working to resolve this mystery, another symptom appeared. I was at the YMCA one afternoon with our daughters, waiting patiently for them to finish their swim lessons. While sitting comfortably on one of the poolside benches, I started experiencing a shooting pain in my mouth. At first, it felt like a canker sore. I had experienced them in the past, so without much concern, I ignored it.

When I got back home, I went directly to the bathroom mirror to examine. To my surprise, I didn't see just one blister, as I had in the past. This time there were numerous, tiny, and painful blisters covering one side of my tongue, and they couldn't be avoided. I didn't worry too much, as I knew they would be gone soon. The next day, to my horror, the other side of my tongue was filled with the same multitude of tiny blisters. I felt the stinging in my mouth all day and all night. Both eating and drinking hot beverages became a problem. I bore this pain for about ten days, still hoping that I would feel better any day. But there was no improvement; the blisters kept coming and coming like a flood. I was miserable; it felt like my tongue and mouth were on a chilly hot fire. I didn't know how to extinguish this fire as there were too many of these little enemies to battle with. In addition, the mucous membranes of my mouth felt tighter and drier too, regardless of how many glasses of water I would drink a day.

My life began to revolve around doctors' visits and lab tests. After examining my mouth, the primary care physician pre-scribed an ointment to numb the blisters which helped me to take hot food and liquids without discomfort for an hour; but it wore off quickly and the pain returned. The worst pain I felt was on the tip of my tongue which continuously had a burning sensation, and even the numbing ointment did nothing to alle-viate it. I was discouraged and disappointed to see that the ointment did nothing to cure this ongoing blister problem.

On my next visit to the doctor, she referred me to an ENT (Ear, Nose, and Throat) specialist who put me through further testing which included a biopsy of the mouth blisters to identify the cause of them. Fortunately, all results were normal, so he suggested I continue to use the numbing ointment and a mouth-wash regularly. I felt such sorrow in my heart during this difficult phase. *Could no one help me? What should I do now since there seemed to be absolutely NO solution for my situation?*

While struggling with the lower body pain and mouth blisters, I tried to get on with my life when another symptom appeared – an extreme form of hyperpigmentation – covering the area around my lips from the outside and inside of the mouth. The black spots that previously appeared on my right leg and back had not yet disappeared, nor did the lighter-shade black mask on the face go away. But now I had to contend with these weird and scary-looking black spots on and around my lips. I felt like a freak and feared that people would shun me. I was trapped in a living hell, and there was no way to escape. I tried so hard, through every medical avenue I knew, to overcome my symptoms but found no certain answers. I thought perhaps the dryness inside my mouth could be the reason for having black spots around my lips. To test this theory, I made an appoint-ment with the director of the Dermatology Department to get counseling regarding this rapidly advancing hyperpigmentation.

After meeting him and running more lab tests, he con-cluded either hypothyroidism or Celiac disease could be the reason for these skin maladies. He suggested I meet with a GI (gastroenterologist) Specialist first and have the doctor deter-mine if, in fact, I had Celiac disease. If the GI doctor ruled it out, the endocrinologist would suggest removing the thyroid (in his words, "kill it") which he believed would take care of the problem. Shobu and I listened to his advice attentively and told him we would need some time to think it over and decide.

At home, my husband and I discussed our next steps and after much thought, we decided surgery was not the answer. We knew my thyroid had issues but felt that killing it altogether and having to depend upon the thyroid medicine the rest of my life wouldn't be a good option. *What guarantee was there that "killing" the thyroid would resolve all symptoms?* Shobu was making this decision for me based on health facts and his scientific knowledge.

We decided to move past the suggestion for thyroid surgery and made an appointment with a gastroenterologist. This doctor had me go through a blood test to check my levels for Tissue Transglutaminase Antibodies (tTG-IgA). In addition, she thought it prudent to perform an endoscopy to be sure there wasn't any damage or inflammation to the lining of my small intestine. Although the endoscopic results showed no damage to the intestinal villi, there was enough evidence from the positive blood test for her to conclude that I, indeed, had Celiac disease. It is an autoimmune disease where the small intestine cannot properly absorb nutrients. When left unchecked over time, it can cause serious problems. There is no cure, but symptoms are alleviated by avoiding gluten, a naturally occurring protein found in several grains, including wheat, barley, and rye.

The gastroenterologist explained that one of the symptoms of Celiac disease is canker sores in the mouth. She advised me to avoid gluten and come back for a follow-up appointment in a year. She made me set up an appointment with a nutritionist who educated me about gluten and Celiac disease and asked me to begin a strict gluten-free diet right away.

After a year, when I went back to the GI doctor for a follow-up appointment, she ordered a second blood test to compare the results of my tTG-IgA levels from the year before, since I had a whole year without gluten. The blood test results showed that my tTG-IgA levels were, in fact, within the normal range. I was glad but disappointed that there had been no change in the hyperpigmentation, the agonizing canker sores, or the dryness in my mouth. Yet the doctor was confident the Celiac disease was under control from the dietary changes. She couldn't explain why the symptoms hadn't abated, and she had nothing more to offer. She recommended I continue with the gluten-free diet. I walked away feeling dejected.

I remained on a gluten-free diet and continued to bear with the symptoms for another year. At the end of this second year, I decided to get a second opinion from a different gastroenterologist. After he reviewed my medical history, he ordered the same blood test I had from the previous two years, as well as an endoscopy. Based on the results from the recent blood work and endoscopy, my new physician simply confirmed that I had Celiac disease and advised me to continue the gluten-free diet and follow-up in a year or two. I felt restricted being on this diet and wondered if this change was worth all the effort to overcome my canker sores and dry mouth problem.

While I continued to do what I was told, I searched to find an alternate cure. One of our family friends spoke highly of a homeopathic doctor residing in Canada. Although this was an expensive route for us, as our health insurance didn't cover his services, we felt it was worth a try. After calling him and explaining my health situation, the holistic doctor immediately put me on an aggressive treatment. Right away, his office began mailing me two-week supplies of the homeopathic pills.

I was familiar with homeopathy, as I had been down that road before. I also knew this treatment was a gradual process, but I was desperate for a solution. Perhaps I should have known that if it didn't work in the past, it wasn't likely to help me now. Nevertheless, I decided to follow my instincts and committed myself to the treatment. Maybe it would work *this time,* I hoped.

While on this holistic path to rid myself of blisters, lower body pain, and hyperpigmentation, I began experiencing stiffness in my lower back which made it hard for me to sit and lie flat on my back, as it brought on additional pain. The only position I could manage was standing. At night, I could only sleep on my side or stomach, but sleep was constantly disrupted due to intense pain. I couldn't move easily at home. This was the worst infirmity I had in my entire life.

I sought help from the homeopathic doctor for this new symptom of stiffness. He prescribed additional medication on top of his originally prescribed pills. After six months, it became clear that this course of action brought no changes or relief. Once again, I lost interest in following this path and gave up on it.

I had no other choice left but to go back and take the painkillers as prescribed by my primary care physician; at least they gave me relief for a short while, which was better than no relief at all. I felt imprisoned in my body and had no idea, nor any options left to find out what was going on with me. Neither the medical or homeopathic doctors could figure it out and come up with a solution. My father-in-law and husband were also helpless in understanding and resolving my health issues. I prayed to the gods and pleaded with them to heal me. Yet, it seemed they didn't hear or see me. I couldn't see any light at the end of this dark tunnel. Questions flooded my mind: *Would I ever come out of my misery? Where should I seek help? Who had the HEALING POWER to restore my physical body and make me well?*

Chapter 13

Embarked on the Path of Lord Krishna

I wasn't ready to face my most dreadful worry - the fear of leaving behind our young daughters without a mom. Without a shadow of doubt, I was confident in Shobu's ability to do a good job raising our girls on his own, but I also knew that being a single parent wouldn't be an easy task for him. That wasn't the issue. My trepidation was about our girls being too young to endure the trauma of losing their mom, and I believed that was going to happen.

There weren't any medical or spiritual options left for me to explore which left me feeling trapped in misery. With Shobu pitching in wherever he could to ease my burden and allowing me time to rest, I could still barely keep up with household commitments. The physical pain and sleepless nights were a nightmare, and I had lost faith that I would be able to make it through the next day.

Our girls were in elementary school at the time, so they were very much dependent on us. My older daughter was part of the Indian Bollywood dance group, which she absolutely loved. She looked forward to her meetings every weekend with this group of girls who were becoming her best friends. The girls were required to practice for at least three months prior to their performance at the major Indian Festival at the Hindu temple. My husband took over the task of getting Anita to practices, so she could continue to partake in her favorite activity. It was a challenging time for our entire family.

Even though driving was difficult for me, I managed to keep up with the girls' swim lessons at the YMCA during the week. As cumbersome as it was for me to walk, I continued to cook, tried to keep the house tidy, kept up with the laundry, and was involved with my kids' academics the best I could. I fought hard to keep things as normal as possible. I lost a lot of weight during this time, unable to savor food in the way that I had in the past. In the back of my mind, I knew I wouldn't be able to carry on much longer with this miserable situation of mine. I feared I would eventually become bed ridden. I felt despondent and didn't know where my help could possibly come from.

At this critical juncture, a Hindu female friend introduced me to a spiritual group which was associated with the religious organization, *Hare Rama Hare Krishna* (HRHK). She came at a time when I thought there was nothing left for me to explore. This religious group believed in and worshipped the Hindu god, Krishna. The guru (teacher) of this group told me that Krishna was the supreme god of all Hindu gods and goddesses, and he blessed those who worship him. When this information came, I thought that I was surely on the right divine path, and I had finally reached what I had sought for so long.

All those years that I was pursuing a connection with and worshipping my family's gods and goddesses, no one ever told me that Krishna was the supreme Hindu god. Now that I was enlightened, I had renewed hope that Krishna was the one who would bring physical healing and release my sufferings. I was certain I had found the answer; I felt remorse that it didn't happen sooner. Questions bombarded my mind: *Why was I not introduced to Krishna along the way when I searched so much? How could I have missed serving the one who could have helped me?* I thanked Krishna for sending a friend to direct my steps and point me to him. Even though I had wasted many precious years worshipping the other Hindu gods, but here Krishna was knocking at my door and reaching out to me.

I was excited to connect with the Krishna religious group, meet with their guru, and make my personal commitment to be part of it. With great enthusiasm, I attended their worship gatherings on Friday evenings. My supportive husband, despite not believing in the same things, attended the meetings with me and our daughters. I met many Hindu families with young children like ours who seemed to be enthusiastic, disciplined, and eager to hear and abide by Krishna's teachings. Our Friday evenings would start with singing bhajans (worship songs) for Krishna, followed by children of all ages reciting their memorized and assigned slokas (scripture verses) in Sanskrit (ancient Indian language), and would end with listening to Krishna teachings from the guru. The entire session would take at least three hours, from 7 to 10 PM. At times, kids were asked to do religious presentations which I thought would enhance their public speaking skills along with their spiritual knowledge.

This Krishna path was brand-new and different from everything I had explored in the past. I was told to adhere to the rigid religious rules and regulations to become Krishna's disciple. I was determined to carry out each one of them faithfully.

I was taught the following discipleship rules:

1. Officially accept Krishna as my god, then wait for the head guru to initiate my discipleship by giving me a religious name and his blessings,

2. Chant Krishna's holy mantra one hundred and eight times per round, as many rounds as possible per day,

3. Refrain from eating any kind of meat or animal products, in other words, change to a strictly vegetarian diet for life,

4. Wear a sacred beaded necklace for the rest of my life,

5. Cook vegetarian food and feed the Krishna statue three meals a day prior to serving anyone in our house,

6. Give Krishna's statue a daily bath, cleanse him, and then put clean clothes on him,

7. Observe Ekadashi fast (auspicious fasting day) twice a month and celebrate Janmashtami (Krishna's birthday) annually, and last,

8. Visit the Hare Rama Hare Krishna temple as often as possible.

Even though this discipleship program was difficult for me to handle due to physical infirmities, I chose to follow through in anticipation that it wouldn't take long for Krishna to make me well. To become a follower, I had to wait a month for their auspicious leader to visit our town. When he finally visited, he asked if I would be willing to be Krishna's disciple and commit to his path. Without any doubt in my heart, I told him, "Yes." Right away, he gave me a spiritual name to be used only in the temple and among his congregation members. I was fine with this.

It didn't take me long to plunge right into the disciple-ship program, and I enjoyed it! I thought I was on the road to recovery, and I would be healed soon and become a brand-new person. This new step in my journey gave me a fresh perspective and assurance for a bright future ahead. It was just a matter of time for things to fall into place, and I believed that it would happen soon.

Up until this point, I was not a vegetarian, but I thought becoming one wouldn't be too much of an inconvenience. My husband, however, was shocked with my proposed plan. He knew this new lifestyle would affect the entire family, particularly changing to a vegetarian diet. I tried to convince him it wasn't as cumbersome as it sounded. I asked him to support me in this decision since Krishna would save my life and bring me out of my misery soon.

Shobu has never been a religious person, rather he is pragmatic in his approach to life. He knew my decision to become a vegetarian wouldn't be feasible in the long run. Against all odds, I stood by my conviction and decided not to eat meat but continued to cook it for my family. This was a huge sacrifice, but I did it diligently.

Moving forward on the Krishna path, I made sure I didn't neglect my religious duties. A typical day started by giving baths to the statues of Krishna and his beloved Radhika (greatest worshipper of Krishna and his constant companion) and dressing them in their clean costumes. After this ritual, I would make fresh vegetarian food for the statues, feed them, and recite the main Krishna mantra one hundred and eight times at least twice a day. Most of the day was occupied in taking care of the deities, reciting mantras, and singing bhajans (worship songs) for them. It was a cumbersome affair.

As challenging as this path was, I tried to keep up with the routine to the best of my ability. My relentless back pain made it difficult for me to carry out the discipleship duties, and I wondered how other devotees followed this time-consuming and all-encompassing lifestyle. I admired their dedication, sincerity, and faithfulness for Krishna.

As time went by, I fell in love with this deity, and I had a desire to know him at a much deeper spiritual level. I devoted my time to reading and understanding his scriptures, worshiping him, and praising him. There were times I would cry for him and request that he would draw me near to him. I didn't have this kind of sentimental relationship with the other deities I served in the past, but Krishna touched and captured my heart. As a result, my love and compassion for him continued to grow.

Despite the exhausting schedule, I kept serving this god without any complaint for the next four months. However, my health deteriorated further, which, of course, made it increasingly difficult for me to keep up with this kind of rigorous schedule. I wondered: *Wouldn't it be easier if Krishna healed and restored me back to good health first, so I could perform religious duties with much ease?*

My bodily pain and lower back stiffness became unbearable, the mouth blisters and their stinging pain persisted, and in addition, I had to contend with sleepless nights. Although daily functions became more and more burdensome, I continued to follow this path until I could no longer adhere to my religious commitment. I questioned Krishna's presence and his demands on my life. In desperation, I contacted the lead guru and explained my health situation in hopes of getting his insight and spiritual advice. Upon receiving my email, he promptly replied and instructed me to continue to keep up with discipleship rules. He didn't encourage or reassure or even mention Krishna being the divine healer. I was saddened by his response, but I didn't question or challenge his faith, nor did I delve into any further spiritual conversation with him.

I was disheartened to realize that the Krishna path was by far the most complicated and challenging of all the other paths I had tried. I concluded if this was the way to reach the highest Hindu god then I would never be able to achieve my goal of coming close to this deity. I started to see how the religious rules and regulations were impossible for me to carry out. Internally, I felt suffocated, not liberated.

I could no longer accept that the highest god, in his sovereignty, would allow his beloved children to endure physical and mental pain, distress, and despair, rather than carve a path of healing, peace, grace, and mercy for them. I came to realize later that Krishna wasn't listening to any of my prayers, just like the other Hindu gods. I questioned: *Why would the highest Hindu god, Krishna, with all his power, not come forth to heal me? Couldn't he see my dire situation with his eyes or hear my prayers with his ears?*

Although I did have admiration and appreciation for those devotees who could pursue this strict regimen, I couldn't see myself and my family continuing with it, especially after six months with no progress. My devotion to Krishna seemed to be a one-sided love, so I chose to discontinue and go no further with the HRHK group. It had not been my answer after all.

Chapter 14

Bittersweet Visit to Michigan

*S*hobu in all his wisdom thought it would be a good idea for the whole family to have a change of scenery, now that the girls had summer break. I was concerned it might be hard on me to travel but thought it would help me focus on something other than my physical distress. We decided to drive up to Cincinnati to see Shobu's parents and do a little sightseeing in the area.

While there, our kids enjoyed spending time with their grandparents, playing board games and outdoor sports like frisbee and soccer, and watching their favorite Disney shows and movies. We also visited the Museum Center at Union Terminal, National Underground Railroad Freedom Center, and enjoyed downtown Cincinnati. One weekend, my father-in-law took us sightseeing in their neighboring city of Lexington, Kentucky. We also got to meet and spend time with Shobu's old friends and their families in Cincinnati. I enjoyed these social interactions and also the meaningful conversations I had with my in-laws, which strengthened our relationship.

During our visit, my in-laws were invited to a non-denominational, coexist religious ceremony in Holland, Michigan, and they asked us to join them. We thought it would be a good idea to expose our children to other religions besides Hinduism and have them learn about others' beliefs and traditions, so we agreed. After our two weeks' stay in Cincinnati, we began our scenic journey to Holland in separate cars. My in-laws planned to head back to Cincinnati the same day, and we planned to spend a couple of days exploring the city.

Once we arrived at the co-exist temple, we greeted other attendees and then went off to explore its sanctuary. The temple also had many rooms, and each one of them was assigned to deities and symbols of different world religions. Our daughters were curious and excited, so they hopped from one room to another and pointed us to various statues of Hindu gods in one room, the symbol of the Cross in another, the statue of Buddha in the next one, and so forth. After they were done with their adventure, we went to the main hall with other attendees to listen to the sermon of the head priest. We were later asked to meditate silently on his teaching for a few minutes, so it could sink into our souls. Toward the end of the service, all the attendees had an opportunity to meet and get to know one another.

The temple also had an interactive room for children where they could explore other religions via puzzles, coloring books, and arts and crafts. Our kids enjoyed spending most of their time in that special room. Later, they were invited to water the temple garden, which had herbs and vegetables. Around noon, everyone was asked to come to the dining hall for lunch, which was prepared by the temple volunteers. It was a delicious vegetarian meal, and we all enjoyed it. We felt blessed to have this friendly and unique experience. When the temple activities ended, we parted from my in-laws and continued our exploration of Holland.

As we drove out of the parking lot, a little distance away on the same street as the coexist temple, we came across a Hindu temple. We decided to stop by to see and compare it to our own in North Carolina. At the front porch of the temple, we noticed a Caucasian woman dressed in Indian clothes engaged in a conversation with another Caucasian woman. It was late afternoon, so their morning service was over, and no one was there in the temple to greet us. We decided to tour on our own.

While we were in the main sanctuary, the two ladies we saw at the entrance came to speak with us. It seemed that one of the ladies was a leader and the other seemed to be her disciple, as the leader carried on the entire conversation with us. She introduced herself as "Yogini," which means a female who practices yoga and meditation. She was inquisitive and asked us personal questions regarding our reason for being in Holland and visiting the temple, particularly since the morning service had ended. It didn't take her long to ask me about the prominent black spots around my lips; she seemed concerned. I felt her compassion and saw she was disquieted by the spots, so I told her I had no idea why or how they appeared on my face. I added that I was under a physician's care in an attempt to get rid of them, but none of the treatments I had tried worked thus far.

Yogini responded by telling us more about herself. She was originally from Yugoslavia but had been living in the U.S. for a long time. She was a Hindu temple volunteer and often participated in its religious activities and events. Additionally, she was a holistic healer and yoga instructor. She had been practicing

Hinduism for over a decade and was heavily involved in transcendental meditation, which helped her "connect to her inner self." She further explained how yoga poses align our body and mind and bring inner healing and deliverance. She then introduced me to her disciple, an American lady, who shared with us that Yogini was her instructor and had indeed helped her to overcome illness.

I had heard about the art of yoga and its physical and spiritual benefits in India, but I was never involved enough to learn much about it. I listened attentively, as her story fascinated me. Yogini offered us a CD which had her recorded step-by-step instructions on different kinds of stretch poses and yoga teachings. She assured me they would be easy to follow if I practiced them at home by myself. Shobu paid her $10 for the CD and wanted to end our conversation there, but Yogini's interest in me continued.

When we accepted the CD, Yogini immediately asked me if she could touch my right wrist to allow her to know what was going on inside my body, and how it was affecting me outwardly, particularly the black spots around my lips. With her strong conviction, I didn't hesitate and offered her my wrist. For a couple of minutes, Yogini held my wrist in her palm while speaking a mantra under her breath. I never questioned it, as I assumed she was reciting a healing prayer over me.

Next, Yogini told me to lay down right where I was on the sanctuary floor, so she could light a tealight candle and put it right beside me. I trusted this stranger and sensed that she only had good intentions toward me. *Who would even think of wishing harm to someone in a Hindu temple?* Her years of experience in the art of yoga and meditation impressed me, and I knew it to be highly regarded in India. I calmly laid down on the temple carpet with my eyes closed, as she instructed. I was asked to relax and rest peacefully until the candle's flame was completely burned out. I did exactly that.

At the end, Yogini gave us her business card and offered her help for any physical or spiritual remedy I might need in the future. We were a bit hesitant but took her card to be polite. She told us that she sometimes visited her clients from out of town, stayed at their house, and did what was necessary for them to overcome their health issues. We said our goodbyes and later reflected on the experience as being odd, but not unpleasant.

After our stay in Holland, we headed back to North Carolina. Within a couple of weeks of our return, I was awakened one morning around 1 AM by cold chills throughout my body. At first, I thought it was a flu symptom, so I bundled myself up well to add warmth to my body. It didn't do anything for me, nor did it allow me to sleep. I laid there and shivered until 4 AM. I checked my body temperature when I got up and was surprised to see that I didn't have a fever, nor did I have any signs of illness. The second, third, fourth – and many nights thereafter – were miserable. The same cold chills would start about 1 AM and last until the early hours of the morning, allowing me only a couple of hours of sleep.

With the onset of this new and strange problem, I didn't turn to medical doctors. I somehow discerned that it had something to do with the lady at the temple in Holland, Yogini. I instinctively felt manipulated by the stranger in Michigan who I trusted. I became afraid she might have tricked me. I wondered if her reason for giving me her business card was to entice me to call her for an opportunity to come to our house. At that thought, I became fearful, thinking she had trapped me in bewitchment.

The chills, along with the sleeplessness, had gone on for two weeks by this time, and I grew more and more anxious. Panic overcame me, as my mind raced through thoughts of a lifetime of nightly chills and disturbed sleep. I was desperate to resolve this new and haunting health issue. I felt my strength and energy being drained from me, but I didn't know where to find relief. I knew that doctors wouldn't understand this situation, as it was a spiritual matter, not a medical one. Although I had abandoned the Krishna path, I decided to contact the lead guru again and ask for his spiritual advice.

Upon receiving my email, he sent me a prompt reply telling me to seek god Krishna earnestly and recite his mantra as many times as I could each day. This alone would help ward off any evil spirits that might be interfering with my body. Since I had no other options, I decided to try it. I thought maybe this time around, Krishna would come forth and rescue me. I wasn't praying for physical healing, just restorative sleep. The cold chills continued to come in the middle of the night, beginning in the upper-mid spine and then spreading throughout my body. Wearing a sweater and covering myself with a blanket in the month of August did nothing to warm me. Once the chills began, they did not leave me until the break of dawn.

At night, instead of tossing and turning to warm myself, I tried to divert my thoughts to Krishna and chant his mantra as long as I remained awake. Another two weeks passed by, but my continued praise and worship to Krishna brought no comfort or peace, nor did it bring me precious sleep. Each night I went to bed, I anticipated that it would be different. Each hour I stayed awake shivering, I asked Krishna to rid me of this frigid nightmare and give me blessed sleep. But Krishna never came forth to rescue me from my distress. It seemed I was pursuing a dead god who could never hear my pleas or see my tears.

I had never heard of cold chills without an obvious cause, and I knew that I couldn't be healthy without adequate sleep. I needed an answer to many questions: *What could these cold chills be? How was it possible that the onset was consistently around 1 AM and their effects disappeared at 4 AM? Most importantly, how and when would I be set free from this torment?*

Chapter 15

A Dead-End in My Life

Since I had a strong sense that my recent health issue was not medical but spiritual, I felt I desperately needed spiritual healing and deliverance. I just didn't know where to go for advice and guidance. Having gotten no help from the lead guru of *Hare Rama Hare Krishna*, it disappointed and upset me. I began thinking about the spiritually inclined people I'd known in the past from whom I could seek guidance. The first connection that came to mind was the elderly Hindu couple who I met in my town many years ago. As our friendship developed, I had many opportunities to hear their insight and knowledge on many religious topics of Hinduism, and I gained an impression they were profoundly rooted in spirituality.

Although we had not been in touch for a long time, I still had their phone number, which luckily hadn't changed. I wasn't sure if they would remember me or be willing or able to assist me, but I decided to take a chance and call them. On my initial call, it was Mrs. Puri who answered the phone. We chatted for a bit and then I talked about my physical symptoms with her. She listened attentively and told me that she would share my experience with her husband who would get in touch with me soon.

After a couple of days, Mr. Puri called and assured me he would look into my problem and help me connect with an experienced and knowledgeable spiritual person regarding my matter. He didn't give me any personal counsel of his own but asked that I would give him some time. He encouraged me to be patient in the interim. Later in the week, he called to let me know that he knew a woman in India who possessed healing power, and he had personally experienced her gift of healing. He passed on her contact number and urged me to get in touch with her. I was grateful for his help and once again, I became optimistic.

Upon calling the Indian healer, Didi, I introduced myself and told her that Mr. Puri referred me. When I described my symptoms, she understood them right away and expressed her confidence that I was in the right hands. She knew how to pray for my healing and assured me that I would sleep peacefully that night without cold chills. Sure enough, that's exactly what happened! When I awoke the next morning after having slept beautifully, I felt relaxed, and oh, so thankful to her! There was no disturbance of sleep, nor were there any cold chills throughout the night and none for many nights thereafter. I stayed in touch with Didi and kept her informed about my situation.

After a week of uninterrupted sleep, the cold chills returned, and my sleep was disturbed again. I wondered, *what could have gone wrong this time?* I contacted Didi and asked her to fix my night symptoms, as she did before. This time, when I reached out, she was positive that she could fix my problem, but it would cost $200. Her fee seemed reasonable, as I felt she was working hard on my behalf. I quickly wired her the money.

Great, I thought, I was back on the road to recovery! Starting the day she received the money, I had a wonderful week of enjoyable and restful sleep, then the chills returned. For the next few days, I went back and forth between restful and sleepless nights. I was hesitant but contacted Didi to complain about it. Outrightly, she asked me to send more money, as the money I'd sent earlier was not sufficient to cover all the expenses for my remedy. I became increasingly leery, but out of despair, I sent her another $200. After she received the money, we began anew with the next few nights being peaceful, then soon the same cycle of having restful and restless nights repeated. After two weeks of the same, I sadly realized that her service gave me only temporary fixes, no matter how much money I sent her.

At that point, it became clear that Didi, the healer, cared little about my distress and didn't possess the divine healing power I had readily put my faith in. I became suspicious that she was a witchcraft doctor and not a healer. Here I thought I was trying hard to untangle myself from the trap of the yoga instructor who I met in Holland, only to fall into another trap with this "doctor of witchcraft." I sensed I was being controlled and manipulated. She certainly wasn't being straightforward about who she really was, and it was painful for me to know that she was not acting in my best interest.

During this time, I talked with my mom in India and told her about my interaction with Didi. I knew Mom had dealt with fake spiritual healers in the past, so she would be able to guide and direct my steps on how to escape from Didi's entanglement. Mom advised me to stop interacting with Didi completely, as she could do me harm with her witchcraft in addition to her being unwilling or unable to help me further. She warned me not to call her or accept her calls. She empowered me with boldness and courage to face this "healer" head on. This renewed confidence replaced my feelings of cowardice and vulnerability, and I immediately cut off all communication with her.

Since I stopped calling Didi and was no longer dependent on her, she would know she had been "found out." I was confident she would leave me alone. I was so wrong. I was genuinely surprised and shaken when I received her first call. Like a stalker, Didi called me at different times of the day and night. At night, I turned off the phone ringer, so her calls wouldn't disturb my family or me. During the day, I was afraid to answer the phone when my caller I.D. displayed her phone number. Despite my unspoken message of no longer wanting to have any interaction with her, she continued to call almost every day. I heeded my mom's advice and did not interact. I was so weary by this constant pursuit that I decided to change our phone number. Though it was inconvenient, it worked, and the calls stopped. What a relief when it ended! I was finally free from her harassment, which took care of one problem, but the cold chills remained unsolved.

This entire incident had a profound effect on my mom. She wanted to be alongside me to console and comfort me, but the long distance between us prevented the physical closeness we both longed for. Mom supported me as much as she could with frequent phone calls, and that was a huge blessing.

Disappointed and scared, I returned to my endless sleepless nights and was defenseless once again. I knew I couldn't continue to endure this night torture. My energy was at an all-time low, and I couldn't be much help to Shobu because of it. He had too many responsibilities on his plate: his full-time job, taking care of the kids when he was home, cooking meals when I couldn't, and running errands for me. I couldn't have asked for more than what he was already doing for our family. He tried not to complain and handled all these extra chores graciously. I didn't want to burden him further with my emotional stress. I felt it would be best to find someone else with whom I could share my inner turmoil and emotions.

I felt I needed a close and caring friend, more than a spiritual healer, someone who would understand and support me. But *where would I find a friend who was of this caliber?* I realized I had already gone to too many people for spiritual advice and remedies in the past. It had in fact made matters worse. None of the healers truly cared about my troubles, nor were they empathetic about the anguish they caused me. I had come full circle in realizing that the healers did not understand me or my situation, nor did they have remedies for my ailments.

This desire to reach out to a true and compassionate friend didn't diminish, but rather grew stronger day by day. After several weeks, the thought of my precious friend, Bindu, suddenly came into my heart. I longed to connect with her, but I buried the idea because we hadn't been in touch for over a decade. Besides, I didn't even know how to find her after such a long silence. But, as the days went by, my longing for connection with Bindu grew stronger and my hesitation grew weaker. One morning, I woke up and was determined to find her. I could hardly wait to hear my friend's sweet voice.

Chapter 16
Reunion with Bindu

After much pondering about how to find Bindu, an idea suddenly popped into my mind. I'd begin a search on Facebook. No sooner had I begun when her profile appeared on the screen. There was Bindu right in front of me, my long-lost friend who had meant so much to me at a time when I was depressed and alone. She looked the same. I had no doubt that she would welcome me back into her life, just as I would welcome her. I immediately rattled off a personal message via Facebook Messenger and asked for her phone number. She responded promptly, and we were once again connected by phone. We were both excited to hear each other's voices! We couldn't talk fast enough to catch up on things.

From that moment, we continued to call every day. Such ease and warmth I felt in her company! After a few days of our bonding over the phone, I opened my heart and shared personal struggles and heartaches with her from the most recent physical symptoms to the old, nearly forgotten ones. She was shocked to hear my story, and what I had been going through for over a decade. She was her old empathetic self, feeling my pain and sorrow through the telephone wires. In addition to empathy, I sensed something more; Bindu's unspoken response was one of assurance, plus a confident optimism for a way out of my problems.

One day, as we continued to catch up, she politely asked, "What have you been doing to overcome your physical ailments?"

I listed all I had done. I saw many experienced and specialized medical doctors in North Carolina, tried various homeopathic treatments, reached out to two Indian spiritual healers, and I cried out to Hindu gods, even the most high, Krishna. All to no avail. Like before, Bindu showed concern, but she didn't seem worried. It was almost as if she was downplaying my plight. This puzzled me, but again, I said nothing. I sensed she wanted to tell me something but was holding back her thoughts for some reason.

Whenever we would talk, I had nothing but complaints about aches and infirmities in my body, the chills at night, a lack of sleep, and a recent new symptom, congestion in my chest, which made it difficult to breathe at times. She listened patiently and continued to support, soothe, and console me over the phone. I was blessed with her friendship again: a divine bosom buddy, soul mate, and friend on my side who I could count on. I was certain I would get out of this gloomy and suffocating place soon, just like I got out of depression back in Houston with her help. I stopped worrying and stressing so much about my current situation. More importantly, Bindu was alongside me and I knew I wasn't fighting the battle alone. What a blessing!

After having heard my moaning and groaning for days on end, Bindu could no longer resist telling me what was on her mind. What she had been withholding burst out as if a gale of wind shot out of her mouth. Bindu's voice changed and became firm. It was loving, make no mistake, but it was like a parent speaking to their child. Bindu began to speak of God and His attributes. She explained that God is supreme and He knows all that I have gone through; nothing has been hidden from Him. I kept listening and thinking about what she was telling me. It did sound like what she told me a long time ago, but this time around, I was more attentive to her wise and honeyed words and took them into my heart.

Bindu knew I didn't fully understand when I, naively, asked, "If the Hindu gods knew all, then why didn't they come to my rescue? Why had they not answered my prayers?" Just as these words left my mouth, it dawned on me that she wasn't talking about "gods" but THE God.

She continued to tell me that God has created us, as He is the Creator of the whole universe, and He knows how to take care of His creation. We are His children, and God does not leave or forsake us in our afflictions, as He is a merciful and forgiving God.

I understood what she said, but it didn't answer my question. I asked again, "If that is true, then why was I forsaken all these years and left to my sufferings and struggles?"

Bindu paused and then reiterated that God never leaves and forsakes us. He is always with us and takes care of us. I attentively listened to her insights about her god and wanted to know more about who this god was. She went on, "God isn't withholding any healing from you, because it is not His divine nature. He is THE Divine Healer and THE Great Physician."

Much of the vocabulary she used about her god was new to me, and I struggled to understand, even when I tried to absorb what she was telling me. She had never spoken to me quite like this before. This spiritual message of hers was more profound than ever before.

Bindu continued, "We as human beings have sinned against God, which has opened the door to many physical, mental, and emotional problems in our lives." She clarified that I wasn't to feel guilty about my personal sins; all of humanity has fallen short, due to our sinful nature. So, when we sinned, we separated ourselves from our very Creator, and that led to our personal demise and destruction.

She further explained, "God gives everyone a free will to make choices, as He is not a forceful God. But He also offers us godly discernment if we seek it, so we may know which path is good or destructive for us. Every action has either good or bad consequences."

"But then doesn't god have the power to take us out of our chaotic and miserable situations?"

"He does, absolutely! God is merciful, gracious, compassionate, kind, and forgiving. God brings us out of our troubles, sets us free, cleanses us from our past sins and mistakes, and transforms us into a brand-new person."

I never heard of this *Eternal Truth* before in the Hindu religion. It sounded too good to be true! There was a huge contrast between what I grew up learning about Hindu gods and their expectations through the process of reincarnation as opposed to what Bindu was telling me about her god. It was starting to make sense as I listened to her carefully with an open mind and heart. I realized I had a lot to explore. Ever since my teenage years I had believed that the supreme Hindu god had the divine power to heal me, liberate me from ailments and pain, and make me healthy and whole. But I had no idea who this god was among the millions of Hindu gods.

I thought I had discovered him when I learned about Krishna but listening to Bindu made me realize I might have missed out on *THE ONE God that* my friend seemed to know so well.

Bindu was born and raised Hindu in India, just like me. She was saying something different now: There is ONE and only ONE Living God of the entire universe, and there are NOT many gods or goddesses as Hindus believe.

I kept going back to my Hindu roots, despite what she was trying to tell me. I was still confused and could no longer resist asking Bindu, "Who is this god?"

She declared with confidence and boldness, "It is no other God than Jesus Christ of Nazareth!"

Chapter 17

My Struggle to Accept Jesus

*W*hen I learned about Jesus at the Presbyterian church in Houston, I thought of Him as a friend, nothing more. I benefited from this feeling; it not only gave me a positive outlook toward life, but it helped calm my internal and external storms. I was satisfied with that back then, but now, with Bindu explaining that He is the Most High God of the universe, suddenly Jesus became a threat to me. *What happened?* How He could change from a friend to a threat with just Bindu's words. I had to ask her, "Why didn't anyone tell me, over a decade ago, that Jesus is the Lord and Savior of all? How could I have missed hearing this most precious fact about Him?"

Bindu didn't shy away from shedding light on Jesus and *who* He is (the one, true, living God) or *what* His attributes are (divine healer, deliverer, redeemer, restorer, forgiver of our sins, and Savior). She was someone I trusted wholeheartedly, and I knew she wouldn't misguide me. I had always listened to her counsel and looked to her for wisdom and insight for situations in my life. But somehow, in these discussions about Jesus, we hit a wall. My heart wouldn't allow me to listen to her passionate descriptions of Jesus. It felt like she had stepped into my personal territory and indirectly insulted my Hindu gods. Her lessons about Jesus were difficult for me to hear, never mind agreeing with, and Bindu understood. Perhaps she had been in the same place herself once.

Bindu, being wise, would impart Jesus' teachings little by little and then wait to see how I would react. Her gentle spirit would ebb and flow based on my acceptance or rejection of God's truth. Whenever she sensed that I was getting overwhelmed with her spiritual knowledge, she would stop and drop the conversation altogether. She would patiently wait for the right opportunity to start back again where we left off. We continued to stay in touch by phone, and I continued to seek advice about my day-to-day deteriorating health and unbearable insomnia. Each time I'd complain and murmur about my ails, she stubbornly pointed me right back to Dr. Jesus, and I found this more and more annoying.

It was no longer uplifting or fun confiding in Bindu. It felt more like a tug of war between her beliefs about *her* God and my beliefs about *my* gods. Our conversations became downright unpleasant, but Bindu continued to stand by me as I continued to complain about stressful times. She persevered despite our challenging and exasperating conversations. She didn't let my stubborn attitude dissuade her, but instead, she kept gently feeding me God's truth whenever she had the chance.

I wondered where her patience came from. If it had been me teaching Bindu, I'd have given up on her when I saw no signs of appreciation for the help I was offering. But Bindu didn't give up. She knew that I didn't understand at the time who Jesus truly was and what He was capable of. Bindu continued to impart and highlight Jesus' characteristics by quoting

Bible verses, ever so softly and lovingly. She started by teaching me what the idols and images of gods signified through the following Bible verses:

Psalm 135:15-18 (New Century Version - NCV)

> "The idols of other nations are made of silver and gold, the work of human hands. They have mouths, but they cannot speak. They have eyes, but they cannot see. They have ears, but they cannot hear. They have no breath in their mouths. People who make idols will be like them, and so will those who trust them."

Leviticus 26:1 (NIV)

> "Do not make idols or set up an image or a sacred stone for yourselves, and do not place a carved stone in your land to bow down before it. I am the LORD your God."

Isaiah 46:7 (English Standard Version - ESV)

> "They lift idols to their shoulders, they carry it, they set it in its place, and it stands there; it cannot move from its place. If one cries to it, it does not answer or save him from his trouble."

Isaiah 57:13 (ESV)

"When you cry out, let your collection of idols deliver you! The wind will carry them off, a breath will take them away. But he who takes refuge in me shall possess the land and shall inherit my holy mountain."

As she continued these unsolicited lessons, Bindu read more Bible verses about God's nature regarding forgiveness, healing, and blessings.

James 5:14-15 (NIV)

"Is anyone among you sick? Let them call the elders of the church to pray over them and anoint them with oil in the name of the Lord. And the prayer offered in faith will make the sick person well; the Lord will raise them up. If they have sinned, they will be forgiven."

Exodus 23:25 (NIV)

"Worship the LORD your God, and his blessing will be on your food and water. I will take away sickness from among you."

2 Chronicles 7:14-15 (NIV)

"If my people, who are called by my name, will humble themselves and pray and seek

*my face and turn from their wicked ways,
then I will hear from heaven, and I will
forgive their sin and will heal their land. Now
my eyes will be open and my ears attentive
to the prayers offered in this place."*

Psalms 41:2-3 (NIV)

*"The LORD protects and preserves them—
they are counted among the blessed in the
land - he does not give them over to the
desire of their foes. The LORD sustains them
on their sick bed and restores them from
their bed of illness."*

As I pondered these verses in my quiet time, everything Bindu shared started to make sense. Yet, there was always this hidden force that would arise and convince me to pay no attention to Jesus. *He's just another ordinary god,* I told myself. *There is nothing special about Him.* These recurring thoughts were a major interference in my ability to accept Jesus. They kept hounding me until I would fall right back to my old beliefs and traditions and turn away from Jesus. I just didn't believe in His healing power, and I continued to seek blessings from the Hindu gods.

During this time of struggle, contemplating who Jesus was and the reasons behind my rejection of Him, it finally became clear to me. I would have to step out of my comfort zone to accept Him, and I couldn't do that. I would have to turn my back on Hinduism, the very foundation of my upbringing. *What guarantee was there that this foreign god, Jesus, would do anything for me?* I was afraid too. *Would I be asked to follow some Jesus-based religious rules and regulations, just as I was asked to do with Krishna?* Lastly, I couldn't bring myself to disappoint my immediate and extended family members by stepping away from Hinduism and divorcing its norms and traditions. In defense of my beliefs, I began pushing Bindu away by telling her there was no difference between Jesus and Hindu gods, as they were all the same, no matter what name we used.

Bindu stood firm in her conviction and shared her own healing testimony with me. She opened herself up and told me that she also had trouble sleeping and continuously suffered from throbbing headaches for many years. She used to take medication to mask her symptoms, which would give her only temporary relief, but when she invited Jesus into her life, she was completely healed.

She further added, "You haven't seen anything like the power of Jesus and His healing miracles!"

Bindu challenged me to find a local church that believed in Jesus' healing power and urged me to ask the pastor to pray for my healing in Jesus' name. She also warned me I should do it as soon as possible before my health would further decline. By this time, I was in pain twenty-four hours a day. Bindu kept on pushing me, but in a caring, gentle, and sympathetic way.

After much pondering, I decided to visit a church that believed in the healing power of Jesus as Bindu suggested. Their service was on a Wednesday night, so I asked Shobu to watch the kids and told him I had to visit someone and would be back soon. I didn't tell him where I was going because I was afraid that I had exasperated him by dragging him through so many health crises – always searching and never finding a cure. Also, I wasn't truly convinced about Jesus' healing power. *Was it even real, and if so, would it work for me? Why tell him if it turned out I would only go to a church one time to receive prayers?*

On that pitch dark, wintry, and rainy night in January 2011, I located the Pentecostal church I had found online. After I parked my car, I quietly entered the church from its back entrance, and slipped in amongst the congregation. I wasn't sure how the church congregants would react to a visit from a stranger like me in the middle of their service. Any stranger in this small church would stand out, and with my Indian looks, it would be obvious that I wasn't a Christian. I wondered: *Would the church folks be gracious and friendly, or even receptive of me, and would they genuinely pray for my healing if I asked?* I decided to put aside my fears and follow Bindu's advice to be present at the service. But soon after I sat down, I found it difficult to pay attention to the pastor's sermon. Sitting for an hour's stretch was cumbersome as my whole body cried out in pain. Nevertheless, I stayed put until the end of his service.

After the service, the lead pastor introduced himself to me and asked if he could be of help. He was easy to talk to, and I told him simply that I was sick. I asked if he would pray for my healing. Without hesitation, the pastor called his wife to join him in prayer. Before he began, he asked me, "Do you accept Jesus as your Lord and Savior?" Although I had no idea at the time what this truly meant or how significant a question it was, feeling it was the right thing to say, and in desperation, I answered, "Yes, I do."

He and his wife invited Jesus to come and heal me. They began their prayers aloud in English, which of course, I understood, but soon their language changed, and I could not understand what they were saying. I sensed, though, that they continued to ask for healing from Jesus, and their foreign language sounded divine. This heavenly language, I later learned, is known as "tongues," one of God's gifts to His children. Instinctively, I knew that their prayers were powerful and magnificent.

I also felt a sudden shift in the church atmosphere. It was no longer the pastor and his wife who prayed for me, but now all the other congregants had joined them in their petition and prayers. Everyone surrounded me like a big family and invited the Holy Spirit (the Spirit of Christ) to come and minister to me. With strong conviction and determination, they prayed for my complete healing and restoration of health. I felt enormous strength and power in their prayers. There was unity and peace among them, and it was all for me! This brand-new experience made me feel blessed and loved.

As they continued to pray, some in English, some in tongues, I felt a caressing breeze that suddenly turned into a strong wind swirling around me and taking hold of me until it completely enveloped me. The wind was so powerful that I could no longer stand on my feet against the force of it. In the next moment, I realized I was no longer standing but lying on the carpet. While lying there, I opened my eyes and looked around briefly. I noticed no one was laying hands on me nor were they even close to where I laid. The congregants were exactly where they stood when they started praying and now they were fully engaged in petitioning for my healing and praising and worshipping the Lord. I saw and heard how forceful they were in their prayers to Jesus on my behalf.

My self-consciousness emerged for a bit, and I suddenly felt embarrassed to be on the floor among these strangers. But the entire experience felt nurturing, inviting, and too good to resist. I continued to stay in this place, and somehow, I knew that I was experiencing the presence of God. The mysterious wind wrapped around my whole body, harder and tighter, like a blanket swaddling a baby. I had no choice but to surrender to this heavenly feeling and remain in the peaceful, restful cradle where I lay. One of the congregants came to cover me with a blanket which lulled me back to sleep and helped me to enjoy this blissful moment.

I tried to stand up once again and join the others, but the weight of God's presence was too powerful for me to stand, and the feeling too great to let it go. I chose to relish it. I could feel an incomprehensible joy in my heart and lightness in my body. Reassured and perfectly comfortable, I closed my eyes once again and was lulled back into supernatural sleep.

After half an hour or so, feeling intoxicated with a sense of well-being, my social awareness pierced through many layers of contentment. I tore myself away from the pure joy of this embrace and gathered my strength to stand. I knew something beautiful and marvelous had just touched every part of me. This experience was new, and I didn't fully understand it at the time. Looking back, I wish I had stayed on the floor as long as God's presence wanted to caress me. It was a sweet, pure, and divine encounter with God, and there was no way to know if I would ever experience it again. *I could only hope and pray that I would have a supernatural encounter like this again!*

Chapter 18

Divine Encounter with Jesus

*E*ven though I felt dizzy after encountering God's presence, I arrived home safely that night. It was getting late, and I knew Shobu would be waiting for me. I didn't talk much, and thankfully, my husband didn't ask any questions. I was left to myself as the kids had already gone to bed, and Shobu was about to retire. The quiet time gave me an opportunity to ponder the supernatural experience I had at the church. I continued to soak up and enjoy God's presence for another hour. I was thankful that I was able to cherish and capture every moment I could with God.

Although I went to bed late, I slept without any disturbance from the cold chills for the very first time in about six months. The next day, I woke up at noon instead of waking up at my usual time of 6 AM. The kids had gone to school, and Shobu had gone to work, so I was alone. As soon as I opened my eyes, I noticed that my body felt refreshed, energized, and at peace! I no longer felt heaviness or pain in my body, and I could move around freely throughout our house. I recognized this new freedom as a blessing from Almighty God.

I immediately called Shobu at work and asked his reason for not waking me up before he left for the office.

He responded, "I tried waking you up several times, but you didn't respond. You seemed to be in a deep sleep, so I decided not to disturb you."

I had no recollection of his attempts to wake me, but I was thankful for his sweetness in letting me sleep because it enabled me to recover some of the many hours I'd lost over the past six months.

All day long, I was in awe. I couldn't take my mind away from the powerful encounter I had with God. I kept thinking; *how did this happen?*

Later in the day, I called Bindu and told her all about my incredible experience at the Pentecostal church. She was thrilled and excited for me. I couldn't thank her enough for pointing me in the direction of Jesus! When I asked for her perspective on my encounter, she told me that I had encountered the Lord's presence – that His Holy Spirit was all around me in the form of the cradling wind. She thought perhaps the Holy Spirit came to give life to my feeble body, so I could experience what it was like to be alive in Jesus. Bindu encouraged me to continue following the path of Jesus, visiting the church, and asking for prayers. I continued to stay in touch with her and updated her on the positive changes the Lord was bringing in my life. She kept cheering me on like I was a champion!

I started to sleep well most nights without interruption, but occasionally, cold chills would return and disturb my sleep. I didn't understand why they would come only some nights, but regardless of this inconsistency, I continued to follow Jesus and be in His church for every Sunday service. After a time, I wanted to tell Shobu about my personal encounter with Jesus, and how it brought me restorative sleep and diminished pain throughout my body. I knew he sensed I was on the road to recovery, as the positive physical changes in me had been obvious to him. What he didn't know until then was that it was Jesus who had touched and healed me, and now was the time to tell him. To my surprise, Shobu didn't make a big deal about my following Jesus, nor did he deter me from going to church on Sundays. I took his quiet acquiescence as a *"yes"* to move forward with Jesus.

That's when I decided I no longer wanted to serve and worship Hindu gods, as they didn't come forth even once to answer my prayers during my thirty-year health crisis. What Jesus did for me in one day was undeniable. I knew it wouldn't be wise or fruitful for me to serve two masters at the same time. It didn't take me long, perhaps a week or two, to start tearing down the home altar. Out of respect, I donated Hinduism scripture books, idols, pictures of gods and goddesses, and their artifacts to a nearby Hindu temple. Maybe it was superstition or an old habit, but I felt an internal fear that if I threw those idols in the trash then the gods would either punish my immediate and extended family or me out of their anger and revenge. As a new-born Christian, I didn't yet know that the Holy Spirit inside me was greater and more powerful than all the other gods I ever served. Looking back, I can see I was still influenced by my familiar past.

Although Shobu never showed much interest in any of our gods or prayed to them, it still came as a shock to him to see our altar being dismantled. I didn't leave any statues in our house. He didn't expect me to act this way, nor did he understand my reasons behind it.

His only comment was, "Why keep these idols anyway, when one can worship god in their hearts without having an image?"

I thank God for the wisdom He bestowed upon my husband which kept him from making a big deal about this drastic act.

Once the idols were gone, and thus, my reliance on them, my attention turned to the next concern: *How was I to worship Jesus?* I was used to reciting mantras, burning incense, and praying to either pictures or statues of the gods, but that wouldn't be the case with Jesus. I asked Bindu who told me I didn't need to worry about having Jesus' picture or His Cross at home or following any rules dictating that I should worship Him in a certain way. Instead, she guided me to read the Bible often to know *who Jesus is* through His Word. She suggested I start reading the Gospels of Matthew, Mark, Luke, and John to have a better understanding of the life of my Savior and to develop a personal relationship with Him.

In addition to Bindu's support, I was able to quickly develop friendships with a couple of women at church. They also suggested that I "fill my mind with God's Word" by reading and meditating daily because it would help me to become a stronger and more mature disciple of the Lord. They assured me that the Lord would answer all my questions and assuage my doubts through His Word. One of them even bought me a Bible, so I could read the Word of God daily.

Grateful for the direction provided, I read the New Testament every day with much enthusiasm. I expected to have a deeper understanding of His Word, but soon found myself getting frustrated as I struggled to get a grip on the meaning of what I read. Just reading the Bible wasn't enough for me; I wanted to comprehend it. When I shared my concerns with my church friends, they simply assured me that if I kept reading, in due time, God would enhance my knowledge of His Word. With renewed determination, I continued the regimen as best I could and read the Bible at least ten minutes a day.

One startling and wonderful result of the days I read the Bible was that I slept soundly at night, without cold chills. They wouldn't dare to come and attack me! On the days I couldn't do my reading, the cold chills returned to haunt me. I couldn't figure out the cause behind this, but it felt like there was a negative force opposing my return to good health. As I continued the journey to read God's Word daily, the dark forces began to lose their grip on my pain, infirmities, and cold chills. This opened my eyes. Not only did Jesus have a profound influence on my healing, but His Living Word carried the same power and authority. It seemed somehow that the evil spirits were afraid to come near me due to the presence of the Holy Spirit and His active Word in my spirit and soul. I was at peace with this new revelation.

Chapter 19

Water Baptism

*O*nce I came to realize that Jesus is the one, true, living, and Most High God, my heart was stirred up to go for water baptism at the church. Water baptism is a symbolic act of Jesus Christ's death, burial, and resurrection. As we enter the water, our former, sinful self dies and is buried just as Christ died and was buried. When we come out of the water, we do so as a brand-new person leaving behind our past sins, shame, and guilt. Our new self becomes alive in Christ just as He rose to life again through the resurrection power of God.

I chose not to discuss my wish for baptism with Bindu, afraid she would tell me I wasn't ready to make this commitment, and I didn't want her to convince me otherwise. At the following Sunday service, the lead pastor announced that there would be a baptism ceremony that day, and he asked us to let him know if we were interested in participating. In that instant, my heart was convinced more than ever, and I boldly expressed my desire for baptism to the pastor. He was pleased to hear and rejoiced with me. The church gave out a long baptismal coat and towels to whoever needed them for their baptism. That eliminated my worry about not having extra clothes or towels from home making it easier for me to do it right there.

As I entered the tub of water and was momentarily submerged by my pastor, a profound divine exchange took place between Hell and Heaven in the spirit realm. In those short seconds, what was of Hell broke off of me, and what was of Heaven was given to me! It felt like that I was no longer an old beaten up and a broken hearted Mamta but a brand-new and hopeful Mamta in Christ. That's the resurrection power of God.

As mentioned earlier, I struggled with the absence of a monthly cycle since the age of thirteen, and received no medical or spiritual cure in India or the U.S. It was a heavy burden for a young woman to carry for three decades, and I had given up hope that this issue would ever be resolved.

However, one day, about two weeks after my baptism, something bizarre, clearly divine, and medically unheard of happened to me. I was startled to see that I began to have periods naturally; rather, I should say "supernaturally." By the time I encountered Jesus, we already had our children, so I was no longer concerned about getting pregnant. I had forgotten about the issue of lack of periods, but Jesus didn't forget my prayers or dismiss my cries and the desire of my heart to be healed. It was shocking news, not just for me, but for Shobu too, as he had never known me to have a monthly cycle in all those years we had been married. That's when I recognized the divine shift which took place during the water baptism. It was the perfect time to share this good news with Shobu.

Later in the week, when I told Bindu about it, she wasn't surprised at all but was familiar with the healing miracles of Jesus. She rejoiced and celebrated with me! Since then, my monthly cycle has been coming on a timely and regular basis. *It was absolutely an extraordinary healing miracle of Jesus!*

The miracle which I experienced reminds me of a woman in the Bible who also had a similar issue having to do with blood. Her story in the book of **Luke Chapter 8:43-44** (NCV) says,

> *"A woman was in the crowd who had been bleeding for twelve years, but no one was able to heal her. She came up behind Jesus and touched the edge of his coat, and instantly her bleeding stopped."*

Prior to meeting with Jesus, this sick and anonymous woman must have suffered a hemorrhage lasting twelve years, which, in those days, made her unclean. Her disease was long standing, yet she was swiftly healed after she touched the hem of Jesus' garment. Her disease lost its hold over her as soon as a divine release of power from Jesus went into her body. She knew and immediately acknowledged that Christ made her whole. That's exactly how I felt when my periods resumed!

Right after this miracle, my hunger to know Jesus grew stronger than ever. It was clear that Jesus is indeed *THE* Miracle-working, Powerful, Almighty God! I experienced His divine touch first-hand over my physical body. I could no longer deny His existence and mighty healing power. Until then, I had absolutely no idea that the solution to my physical, emotional, and spiritual issues had been all along in Jesus' hands. *Wouldn't it have been wonderful if I had been introduced to Jesus and His miracle working power when I was a teenager?*

Chapter 20

My Initial Walk with Jesus

During the first six months after accepting Jesus, I cherished spending intimate time with Him and loved talking about Him to my friends and relatives. Toward the end of this phase, I had another divine encounter. One Sunday while I was worshiping Jesus in a kneeling position at the church altar, a precious sister-in-Christ came right behind me, laid her hands on my back, and prayed for me for at least thirty minutes in her divine language. Although my knees got tired in this one position, I chose to stay put and decided not to interrupt her. As she continued to pray, my mouth started to mumble in some sort of language that I didn't understand. It sounded strange at first, but I knew I had received the baptism of the Holy Spirit from Almighty God!

The church congregants witnessed and confirmed I was indeed filled with the Holy Ghost (Holy Spirit) by the utterance of God's divine language. Everyone in the church rejoiced and celebrated alongside me. It was an amazing spiritual experience, and I was thankful to my sister-in-Christ who prayed earnestly and enthusiastically to the Lord for me. I didn't know the meaning of any of the heavenly words I spoke, but they came out beautifully from my mouth and sounded divine.

By then, I was already sleeping soundly, the revolving pain between my waist and feet had disappeared, and the stiffness and pain in the lower back were no longer an issue. Above all, my periods resumed regularly. At my next six-month follow-up appointment with the endocrinologist, it was confirmed through my blood tests of T4, T3, and TSH that I no longer had hypothyroidism. My blood test results came back in the normal range for the first time without the help of kelp. When my doctor asked if I was still taking kelp, I disclosed to him that I had quit taking it six months prior, ever since my periods became normal. In the past, other doctors told me that hypothyroidism was the cause of my missing periods, but since this was not an issue anymore, I chose to discontinue kelp on my own. The doctor was surprised to hear my story, but the blood tests were enough evidence for him to tell me to keep doing what I had been doing. He congratulated me and told me I didn't need to make any further appointments with him unless the annual blood work indicated a change in my thyroid numbers. I had "graduated" from the endocrinologist's care which was yet another miracle!

For the first time in my life, I felt I was on the right track with *THE* True God, *THE* Divine Healer, and *THE* Great Physician, Dr. Jesus. What joy! What a relief! No more knocking on doors of faith healers or medical or homeopathic doctors! As my physical body underwent the process of recovery and repair, my life returned to normal. I was able to handle more responsibilities and do more chores than I had been able to in years. Shobu was less burdened and worried about my health. The girls could sense a shift in our home atmosphere, as there was more joy, harmony, and happiness all around us. I couldn't contain the liveliness and love Jesus brought into our lives, and I had to share it with the world. I told people about Jesus, my personal divine encounter with Him, and the healing which I had received from Him. I am forever grateful for what Jesus did for me and the blessings He bestowed upon me!

As I relished this new-found sense of well-being, my focus returned to the less concerning ailments like the recurring mouth blisters, stinging pain at the tip of the tongue, continuous shedding of hair, and the hyperpigmentation of skin. I was confident and patient that the rest of my healing would come at God's appointed time. In the meantime, I simply rejoiced and kept giving Jesus praises and more praises!

My faith in Jesus' healing power grew stronger, and I knew it was only a matter of time before everything else would fall into place. I simply surrendered my will to the Lord and waited patiently with contentment for other miracles to happen. I also felt a nudge in my heart that I was not alone in the spiritual fights anymore, as Jesus was with me every step of the way. He was the one who was fighting against the enemy of my soul, the devil, who brought so much havoc, pain, suffering, and infirmity to me.

There were still days and nights the enemy tormented me physically by bringing back some old symptoms, including the ones Jesus had already delivered me from. He tried to convince me that Jesus didn't really do anything for me, as my past ailments weren't gone but remained a stronghold over my body. Instinctively, I knew I needed help to overcome this battle in my mind.

Upon sharing my concerns with Bindu, she encouraged me to read the Word of God daily, as this alone would be my spiritual weapon and protective shield against the enemy. She helped me understand that the battle was truly between God and His enemy, the devil, and in the end, God would win over His foe. She further explained that the devil was lurking and waiting to see when I was vulnerable, so he could bring chaos, confusion, and distraction against me. The enemy would try hard to hold on tight, so I wouldn't be set free from his grip.

Bindu assured me that the battle belonged to the Lord, but I had to do my part, which was to stand strong like a warrior and rebuke the devil every time he would bring back my old symptoms or torment me with his lies. She reiterated the truth that Jesus had already healed me; I had to stand firm on this conviction. If I were to accept the devil's lies and come into an agreement with him, he would win; but if I agreed with God's Word, I would experience God's victory instead. This was an important spiritual lesson and a sustaining truth I embraced early on, thanks to my friend.

Bindu told me the Lord might restore my health little by little, so not only I could handle the wholeness in my body but also be able to maintain it. It was one thing to receive healing from Him, but I could lose it if I didn't learn how to steward it well. She explained that we are made up of three parts: body, soul, and spirit. The body is the physical structure of a human being, but the soul is made up of our mind, will, and emotions and is the essence of who we are as a unique individual. Our human spirit comes alive when God's Holy Spirit dwells in us which happens right after we get saved and accept Jesus as our Lord and Savior.

Bindu made an analogy by comparing our human soul to an onion. Just like an onion has many layers, so does our human soul. It's the Lord's job to peel back our soulish layers, one at a time, as He alone knows what traumatic, negative emotions and thoughts have been embedded in our wounds.

As He would peel, He would also heal, and in due time, He would bring complete restoration to my soul which would positively affect my body.

As I pursued the Lord to receive more healing, He highlighted deep, open wounds in my soul which were yet to be cleansed, closed, and covered with His healing balm. It was clear that only the Lord could drive the darkness out from them and then fill those dark recesses with His truth and light. For this to happen, I had an important commitment to make which was to obey Jesus and not interfere with His healing process. Although I had no idea how long Jesus would keep me in His protective cocoon, I wholeheartedly trusted His course of action and timing. Curiosity made me wonder: *What kind of beautiful butterfly would I emerge into, and how would it transform my life thereafter?*

Chapter 21

Golden Keys to Unlock the Healing

*U*nbeknownst to me, Jesus had only scratched the tip of the iceberg when He healed my physical ailments. Being able to sleep well and overcoming the pain that radiated from my waist to feet were my primary concerns, but apparently not His. Jesus knew about other hidden factors which contributed to many other ailments, although I was not even conscious of them. Because I had struggled with them all my life, I had learned to live with them. Since they were out of my mind, overcoming them was no longer a priority for me. Jesus, however, forgets nothing; He saw all that I had endured. He knew my soul was fragmented, and His intervention was needed for it to be mended, healed, and restored.

I was excited to embrace Jesus' healing journey, even though I didn't have the slightest clue what I would expect along the way, or what each deliverance and restoration step might look like. The one important thing which resonated in my heart was that this embarkation was divine and God-led, and it would ultimately take me into the open space of freedom, wholeness, and health I so longed for. I felt no apprehension;

I knew there was no risk in this experience with Jesus. Even though His path was new to me, I was a bit familiar with it because of my first-hand divine experience with God at the Pentecostal church. Right from the start, there was a strong pull in my heart that I was to rely on His Holy Spirit at every step of the healing process. I knew Jesus was *THE ONE* carving this path, and all I had to do was to follow His footsteps and be obedient to His lead.

Be a Good Steward of God's Word

My initial lesson from Jesus didn't come as a surprise. I knew His desire was for me to be His faithful student and be grounded in His living Word, so I could fully know Him and His attributes. Through the Gospels of Matthew, Mark, Luke, and John in the New Testament, I learned about *who* Jesus is (the one, true, living God), *what* His true nature is (a divine healer, redeemer, restorer, forgiver of sins, comforter, just judge, provider, mediator, savior, and counselor), and *what* His reasons for dying on the Cross for all of humanity were (to set us free from our personal and generational sins, diseases, iniquities, strongholds, and eternal death).

As I spent time reading God's Word, the Holy Spirit highlighted scriptures to me from both the Old and New Testament. Jesus wanted me to not only understand the reasons behind my physical pain and infirmities, but also embrace the solutions for them through His healing promises mentioned in the Bible. Under the Holy Spirit's guidance, I understood it wasn't God who brought diseases, but the enemy of my soul, the devil himself.

I now knew that Jesus, *THE* Divine Healer, would never retract His healing nature. He was not the one who left me to endure pain for three decades. This was a brand-new biblical truth I learned early on about Him, and I was glad I did.

John 10:10 (NIV)

> "The thief comes only to steal and kill and destroy; I have come that they may have life and have it to the full."

It was one thing for me to read and know His truth, but it was another thing to continuously *meditate* on His Word, which was vital to my inner healing and deliverance.

I took away a key point, one that was as precious as gold to me, and has served me well throughout my life. I sensed that more were coming, so I named this one, "Golden Key #1."

Golden Key # 1

Knowing Jesus and His truth, and renewing my mind continuously with His Word was the First Golden Key to my healing and deliverance.

Confession, Repentance, and Forgiveness

Jesus made me understand that for every problem we face in our lives, there is already a solution given in the Bible. We just need to dig deeper into God's Living Word and find divine answers for our problems. We can also inquire directly from Jesus, as He is gracious to provide them to us.

The Lord highlighted Bible verses from the book of Deuteronomy which delve into the topic of generational blessings and curses.

Deuteronomy 5:9-10 (NCV)

> *"You must not worship or serve any idol, because I, the Lord your God, am a jealous God. If people sin against me and hate me, I will punish their children, even their grandchildren and great-grandchildren. But I will be very kind for a thousand lifetimes to those who love me and obey my commands."*

Upon meditating on this verse, I became aware that future generations inherit the outcome, good or bad, from their ancestors. Sins that remain unconfessed and unrepented of before God bring serious consequences not only to those who committed the transgressions, but to those who come after. Unless, or until, someone in the family line stands before God, repents, and asks for His forgiveness, the sin remains sin, and therefore, generation after generation suffers as a result.

People may still raise the question: *Didn't Jesus take care of all of our sins, strongholds, and iniquities on the Cross when He died for us?* Yes, He did, but it is important for us to personally receive and appropriately apply all that Jesus did on the Cross. If the Holy Spirit prompts and points out any of our ancestral and personal sins then we should follow His lead, confess, and repent to God. By doing this, we can receive His forgiveness, cleansing, healing, and deliverance from all those wrongdoings committed either by us or by our ancestors against Him.

1 John 1:9 (NCV)

> *"But if we confess our sins, he will forgive our sins, because we can trust God to do what is right. He will cleanse us from all the wrongs we have done."*

Our sins might include idolatry, adultery, fornication, addictions, wrath, violence, pride, witchcraft, occultism, greed, and so on. With the help of the Holy Spirit, I was able to make a note of many visible and obvious strongholds in my immediate and extended family. *Idolatry* (worshipping idols and statues) on both sides of my parents' families was one of the prominent sins which stood out right away in addition to many others. *Occult practices* (seeking advice from faith/spiritual healers, relying on horoscope, palm, and tarot card reading) were other sins that grabbed my attention. I understood that the enemy would very likely take advantage of these unconfessed sins if I didn't address them through a prayer of confession and repentance to God.

Jesus further highlighted similar physical symptoms that my first cousins on my mom's side endured: hormonal imbalance, thyroid disease, irregular periods, and thinning hair. That's when I recalled my cousins' conversations from many years before discussing their hormonal problems. I didn't make a big deal about it or even pay much attention to their concerns at the time. But after receiving this new revelation about generational sins, my first thought was: *How unfair and painful that my cousins and I had to bear the ramifications of our ancestors' sins?* Medical doctors would call it "genetics" and refer to it as our "family history," but it became clear to me that the hypothyroidism and barrenness I suffered were the unresolved consequences of some sort of generational sin in my family line.

To continue Jesus' healing path and receive more healing and freedom from Him, the first and foremost task was for me to let go of my ego and pride and confess to Almighty God that my ancestors and I indeed sinned against Him, intentionally or unintentionally. This was a big but very important step for my healing. It wasn't that I took responsibility for my ancestors' sins, but I acknowledged them, repented on their behalf, and asked for God's forgiveness. This simple act of obedience, and the childlike faith it required, was one of the keys which led to my freedom through Christ.

Golden Key # 2

Verbal confession, repentance, and asking for God's forgiveness of my ancestral and personal sins was the Second Golden Key to my healing and deliverance.

Fight Offensively

During my entire "healing" journey with the Lord, the enemy didn't stay quiet. In fact, he brought torment against my soul to make me feel frustrated, baffled, and discouraged. The enemy indeed tried hard to persuade me to listen to his lies and adopt them as my own. At times, my mind would be filled with thoughts like *I wasn't really healed; my old symptoms had come back; my healing was only a temporary fix,* and so on. I learned to shake off these deceptive thoughts, and in its place, I actively filled my mind with God's truth.

I also learned to wage war, not defensively but offensively, against the fiery darts the enemy flung at me. This rigorous "boot camp" training helped prepare me, not only to know God's biblical principles, but also to use them mightily as weapons of warfare against the adversary. The enemy never plays fair with any of us; he would surely have been an impediment to my complete healing...if I had allowed it.

Jesus knew we would be fighting many spiritual battles together before I would be occupying my promised land of freedom and health. I had no other choice except to be ready wearing the full armor of God and to remain steadfast in the face of my opposition, oppression, and adversity. The shield/armor of God is defined in the book of Ephesians:

Ephesians 6:13-17 (NIV)

> *"Therefore put on the full armor of God, so that when the day of evil comes, you may be able to stand your ground, and after*

you have done everything, to stand. Stand firm then, with the belt of truth buckled around your waist, with the breastplate of righteousness in place, and with your feet fitted with the readiness that comes from the gospel of peace. In addition to all this, take up the shield of faith, with which you can extinguish all the flaming arrows of the evil one. Take the helmet of salvation and the sword of the Spirit, which is the word of God."

I learned that the way we stand against the enemy says a lot about our confidence and who we are in Christ. Our identity in God comes from seeing ourselves as He sees us, finding our worth in Him, and knowing and acknowledging what He has already done for us on the Cross through His Son, Jesus Christ. This important lesson was the next key in my healing journey.

Golden Key # 3

Fighting offensively instead of defensively against adversaries was the Third Golden Key to my healing and deliverance.

Acknowledging Our Hurts and Pains

Another area the enemy fought hard against me was my life's unresolved hurts and pains. We all face this, like when someone hurts our feelings or when we experience disappointments or failed expectations or when we are judged or criticized by others. There are times we may even compare ourselves with others and feel envious of them. All these experiences can lead to feelings of bitterness, anger, jealousy, fear, guilt, unforgiveness, frustration, unbelief, and so on.

For a long time, I held bitterness and anger against those who either criticized me verbally or intimidated me by their actions. I also internalized their derogatory remarks and took them to heart, which hurt me deeply. As a result, I held onto unforgiveness toward them. Also, there were times I compared myself to others whose personal and professional achievements seemed greater than my own. It inadvertently brought insecurity and an inferiority complex in me. Instead of dealing with these incidents as they occurred, I tucked them away in my heart and mind for a long time, so they became part of me.

Through the healing journey, I understood that these distresses drain the life out of us and can affect us in every area of our lives. Pain can stifle and shut us down completely. For a short time, we can easily block our ache to get rid of it, which is what I did; but over time, these bottled-up feelings steal the abundant life and joy God intends for us. Hurts which are not acknowledged, cannot be healed.

God will not willfully touch the bruised places of our lives unless and until we invite Him in and give Him our permission to deal with them. We have an important role to play here, and it begins with us asking for the Lord's help. We must let Jesus speak, and we must hear what He has to say to us personally about each of our distressing situations. Sometimes Jesus will point out when we have acted wrongly toward others, so we could ask and receive the Lord's forgiveness for others' hurt. Other times He will give us His truth, so we are able to change our thinking and renounce the lies we have previously accepted about the character of a person, either by listening to gossip or making judgments about a person.

I learned that evil spirits could access our lives through unhealed wounds from either personal traumas or hurtful situations. Our negative responses, whether they be lashing out, withdrawing, being offended, or withholding forgiveness are what make it easier for demons to have access to us. If the enemy can penetrate our soul, we remain vulnerable to his influence, and it becomes almost impossible to escape from his grip. Hence, we remain bound to our misery and inadvertently block our healing from God.

Unless we get to the root cause behind our hurts and pain – and we need God's help with this – demons remain in control and bring turmoil and havoc into our mind, body, and emotions. Once healed, demons have no choice but to flee from our soul; they are rendered helpless to torment us any longer. The fact is that Jesus is always standing by our side to overcome our agonizing circumstances, whether or not we feel or recognize His presence.

John 16:33 (NIV)

> "I have told you these things, so that in me you may have peace. In this world you will have trouble. But take heart! I have overcome the world."

Demonic powers are no match for the name and authority of Jesus Christ. Demons only get an upper hand on us when *we* break God's law, allowing the enemy free reign to torment and oppress us. God's expectation for all of us is simple: *We must acknowledge and repent for our sins, and we must also forgive others.* When we follow this command, then, and only then we are set free. It is like the analogy of our breaking traffic laws and getting a ticket. We are summoned to go to court either to petition our case or accept responsibility for our guilt and pay a fine. Once we take care of it, we are released from further consequences.

Our sins and wrongdoings deserve punishment, sometimes more severely than we realize, but Jesus does not treat us harshly. Out of His love, compassion, and mercy, He forgives our sins and remembers them no more upon our confession. He even removes the stain of our sins, cleanses us from all unrighteousness, and purifies us, so we become a brand-new person in Him.

Psalm 103:10 (NCV)

> "He has not punished us as our sins should be punished; he has not repaid us for the evil we have done."

As I studied the following Bible verses, it became clear that forgiveness is the key to overcoming our hurts and pain, as it sets us free from imprisonment.

Ephesians 4:31-32 (NIV)

"Get rid of all bitterness, rage and anger, brawling and slander, along with every form of malice. Be kind and compassionate to one another, forgiving each other, just as in Christ God forgave you."

Matthew 6:14-15 (NIV)

"For if you forgive other people when they sin against you, your heavenly Father will also forgive you. But if you do not forgive others their sins, your Father will not forgive your sins."

Luke 6:37 (NIV)

"Do not judge, and you will not be judged. Do not condemn, and you will not be condemned. Forgive, and you will be forgiven."

In God's perfect time, He unveiled to me several traumatic events from my past and had me deal with them one at a time. God did it with precision by taking me back in time to the places where the events occurred, so that there was no mistaking. God knew all my pains and hurts, whether they came from my former boss not appreciating me, being misunderstood,

GOLDEN KEYS TO UNLOCK THE HEALING

judged by others, or being betrayed by the ones in whom I confided. He noticed them all and helped me to forgive others.

There is no formula I can explain as to how Jesus ministered to me. I simply sat still and waited for Him to touch each one of the wounded areas of my soul where His healing was needed. As He would open those wounds, I could feel the pain again and experience the blow of each disappointment, and I would taste the bitterness and sting of anger. But in the midst of all of this, I trusted the Lord completely and His restorative process in bringing freedom and divine healing to me.

Psalm 147:3 (NCV)

> *"He heals the brokenhearted and bandages their wounds."*

After each healing encounter, I felt God exchange my mourning for joy, my ashes for beauty, my hatred for love, and my hopelessness for hope. At the end, the bonds of my captivity gave way to liberating enlightenment! Jesus exchanged all the lies I had believed – lies I told myself and lies that were told to me – with His truth. It became clear that the unresolved pain in my soul contributed to my sickness and kept me in captivity for so long. I never knew it was my responsibility to take my hurts and pains to the Lord and have Him deal with them one by one through a simple prayer of repentance and forgiveness in Jesus' name.

As I began the process of genuinely forgiving those who hurt me, releasing them from my heart, and blessing them, it brought healing to every part of my being. Jesus even asked me to forgive myself and release to Him those toxic emotions toward others that I had held on to so tightly. As I carried out these steps, it brought incredible relief and freedom. The hardness in my heart toward those who hurt me was now softened with empathy and love. Even my mind felt liberated once toxic thoughts were gone.

Proverbs 10:12 (NIV)

> "Hatred stirs up conflict, but love covers over all wrongs."

Proverbs 28:13 (NIV)

> "Whoever conceals their sins does not prosper, but the one who confesses and renounces them finds mercy."

I was enlightened to know this fact that it is us, not the offending person, who stays bound if we don't let go of our offenses against others and release them to Almighty God who is the fair judge of all. I also learned that Jesus is more than happy to carry our burdens of worry, anxiety, guilt and shame. In return, He wants us to carry a lightened burden of trust and belief in Him. *What a beautiful and divine exchange of yokes between Jesus and us!*

Matthew 11:28-30 (NIV)

> "Come to me, all you who are weary and burdened, and I will give you rest. Take my yoke upon you and learn from me, for I am gentle and humble in heart, and you will find rest for your souls. For my yoke is easy and my burden is light."

Golden Key # 4

Acknowledging my hurts and pains, forgiving others genuinely, and letting go of negative emotions was the Fourth Golden Key to my healing and deliverance.

Breaking Self-imposed and Others' Curses

Word curses, both self-imposed and those spoken by others, were the next area that Jesus brought to my attention. I had no idea that these curses, just like our sins, could bind us for life until we take a stand against them in Jesus' name. When the Holy Spirit brought to my attention the negative words spoken over me either by others or by my own lips, I was directed to nullify and reject them. That's when I understood that God's Word activates blessings, and the devil's word activates curses. Heaven and Hell are hearing our words simultaneously, and they each bring about different results depending on what we speak over ourselves and how we react to what others say. We have freedom to "feed ourselves" with either positive or negative words. This was a valuable gold nugget I received from the Lord!

I embraced this lesson and realized that we open our lives to curses when we give credence to them. Sometimes we agree simply by not refuting them, thus allowing them in. As we accept and believe these negative words, they dictate our thoughts which dictate our actions, and our actions carve the path to our destiny. I remembered when I was depressed at seventeen about losing my hair, I would often speak critically of myself, *"I will become bald soon, I will have to wear a wig. I look ugly compared to other teenage girls."* I learned that my self-destructive words not only brought sadness and hopelessness into my life, but they made me bear the bad result of hair loss and depression.

Proverbs 18:21 (NIV)

*"The tongue has the power of life and death,
and those who love it will eat its fruit."*

Jesus directed me to take authority over those self-binding curses and break them off in His name. I followed His lead and did exactly what He asked me to do. Instead of the negative language I had once used over my hair, I now commanded, *"Let my hair be healed and restored back to its God-given order in Jesus' name. Let every strand of my hair and its follicles be anointed and covered with the blood of Jesus. Let it grow thicker, stronger, and longer than ever before in Jesus' mighty name!"* Sure enough, my hair responded!

During the days following my new positive decrees, my hair began the process of becoming healthier and more vibrant. I could see the difference right away; it was no longer shedding as much. As I continued to command and simultaneously bless my hair, it stopped shedding altogether and began to grow thicker than ever. I realized that my past negative words had power and authority over me which prevented me from receiving the very best God had for me.

As further led by Jesus, I rebuked and cancelled every negative word ever spoken over other areas of my life. I now spoke life and blessings over circumstances that had previously been labeled dead and were called cursed. My continual positive decrees and declarations brought tremendous healing and restoration to many areas of my life!

Job 22:28 (King James Version - KJV)

> *"Thou shalt also decree a thing, and it shall be established unto thee: and the light shall shine upon thy ways."*

Jesus has given us the power to nullify and abort every word which doesn't align with His Word and Truth. We must be mindful of what we speak over ourselves and others, for words are powerful and carry mighty weight.

Matthew 12:37 (NIV)

> *"For by your words you will be acquitted, and by your words you will be condemned."*

Golden Key # 5

Breaking curses, whether self-imposed
or spoken by others, in Jesus' name,
was the Fifth Golden Key to my healing
and deliverance.

Reject Ungodly Thoughts

The next area I needed to learn was to check my "thought life," something I had never even considered, yet the mind is precisely where most of our battles are fought. I could win or lose depending on which thoughts I discarded and which ones I accepted. I realized that the enemy attacks our mind with deceptive thoughts, plays with our emotions, and pressures us to surrender to *his* will instead of God's will. If we pay attention to his deceptive schemes and enticements, then we are going to be trapped in his net and may stay there for a long time. This was my situation until Jesus came into my life and set me free with His truth.

I didn't realize that I was making myself susceptible to the enemy and playing right into his hands when I was entertaining anxious, worrisome, and fearful thoughts. If I had continually accepted these ungodly thoughts, they would have eventually driven me away from God's truth. I understood that our thoughts form our beliefs. As we believe, we become. So, my questions were: H*ow should I protect myself from these unwanted thoughts in the first place, and how do I dispel them after they enter my mind?*

I learned that it was *my* responsibility to keep my thoughts in check by renewing my mind daily with the Word of God. Rather than leaning on my understanding and wisdom, I could depend upon God's counsel, instruction, and direction over my thought life. Meditating on God's Word helped me to discern which thoughts were from God and which were from the devil.

Proverbs 3:5-6 (NIV)

"Trust in the Lord with all your heart and lean not on your own understanding; in all your ways submit to him, and he will make your paths straight."

Similarly, I must not entertain any of the enemy's demeaning opinions about other people. This creates barriers as well as animosity. When Jesus led me to examine this, I knew that I did not want to be part of it, not only for my sake but for others' as well. I understood that I must use godly discernment now that I was aware of this new-found danger. I should not partake in certain discussions because gossip may be disguised as conversation. We should be aware of what we allow in our lives because everything we let in, without filtering it through God's lens, has an influence on us. When we stop judging others, and start judging ourselves instead, pride goes out the window.

Matthew 7:5 (NIV)

"You hypocrite, first take the plank out of your own eye, and then you will see clearly to remove the speck from your brother's eye."

James 4:11 (NIV)

"Brothers and sisters, do not slander one another. Anyone who speaks against a brother or sister or judges them speaks against the law and judges it. When you judge the law, you are not keeping it, but sitting in judgment on it."

Golden Key # 6

Staying focused on God's truth, and refusing to entertain ungodly thoughts was the Sixth Golden Key to my healing and deliverance.

Become the Warrior God Has Called Us to Be

Jesus' healing path required me to be patient, persistent, and persevering in facing the obstacles and hardships which came along. There were times the enemy pushed me to the edge by either intensifying my bodily symptoms or bombarding me with negative thoughts like my healing wouldn't come or I would never come out of my valley of despair. These attacks made me want to quit and forfeit my firm stand against the enemy. If I had given in to the devil's tactics and taken my eyes off from Jesus during the spiritual battle, I would have slid right back into the place of darkness and turmoil where I was once. Despite trials and tribulations, I kept on moving forward toward the finish line.

I remember when the devil brought back the old maddening night chills after I was completely healed and set free from them. Night after night, for seven days, I had no peace and no sleep. On the eighth night, when I could no longer stand it, I began to doubt: *Maybe Jesus hadn't healed me after all.* I came close to yielding to the devil and forfeiting my newfound freedom. That's when the Holy Spirit reminded me of my identity in Jesus. He helped me grab a hold of my God-given authority and spiritual weapons so that I could fight a good fight against the adversary and see him to flee from me. Since that day nine years ago, the cold chills have not returned. This God-given endurance and perseverance strengthened me to become the warrior God wanted me to be.

James 4:7 (NCV)

"So give yourselves completely to God. Stand against the devil, and the devil will run from you."

Another time, the devil brought me a severe stomachache which lasted several days, until I was nearly convinced my Celiac disease had returned. This time, I had to remind myself that I was indeed set free from Celiac disease as confirmed by my gastroenterologist two years ago. The physician knew, of course, that this disease has no cure, as it is a lifelong condition. When he declared me free from Celiac disease, he said, "You are blessed."

The Holy Spirit made me realize that these symptoms I experienced were the enemy's ploy to lure me back into the captivity of Celiac disease upon my acceptance of it. Once I understood this new revelation from God, I resolved my stomachache issue by speaking aloud God's truth to the enemy that my stomach had been already healed in Jesus' name. I then commanded my stomach to come in alignment and agreement with the Word of God and be restored back to its God-given order. Sure enough, my body responded, and healing came swiftly. These were a couple of the many tough lessons of perseverance and persistence I learned during my healing journey with the Lord.

There were times I stayed in the valley of agony for a short time; other times I was there longer, but I recognized this was God's way of teaching and preparing me to become a strong warrior. These kinds of stumbling blocks helped me to become mature in my faith, made me dependent on Jesus, and encouraged me to trust His unfailing love and faithfulness. The important fact which has stayed with me to this day is that if God had brought me out of valleys in the past then He would bring me out again. This is how we grow spiritually and move from one level of faith to another. We Christians call this process "spiritual transformation and sanctification."

I realized I had nothing to fear, as Jesus was walking alongside me, backing me up every step of the way, and leading me toward the invigorating and thriving life He had for me. He also taught me how to be tenacious in my pursuit, so I would not only tire the enemy out but would eventually defeat him in his endeavors to steal, kill, and destroy my blessings of the Lord. This rigorous training molded me to become the spiritual warrior I am today.

Golden Key # 7

Staying persistent in the midst of spiritual battles was the Seventh Golden Key to my healing and deliverance.

The Seven "Golden Keys" are gifts from God, and they are effective and mighty weapons of the Lord! These Golden Keys not only brought divine wisdom, knowledge, and understanding to me personally, but they've also helped me to permanently shut the door on the devil in areas where I used to be unshielded. This healing journey not only helped build my faith muscles but made me grow stronger in the Lord.

These keys are not the result of human effort, but of revelation from the Holy Spirit. They unlock permanent healing for all who ask and are free to all who seek Jesus. Simply put, we must let the Holy Spirit, God's spirit in us, lead and guide us in every sphere of our lives and provide the solutions we need for our lives.

Matthew 16:19 (NIV)

> *"I will give you the keys of the kingdom of heaven; whatever you bind on earth will be bound in heaven, and whatever you loose on earth will be loosed in heaven."*

Epilogue

I am beyond blessed to know the Gospel of Jesus Christ which has brought so much freedom, peace, and order in my life. All along, Jesus was the answer to my life-long problems. He was only waiting for me to come to Him. I thank God for not letting me give up in my determination to seek Him until I found Him. My three decades of searching in so many different places for physical healing helped me instantly recognize Jesus, the Divine Healer, at the Pentecostal church. Upon my personal encounter with the Lord, I was immediately set free from excruciating body pain and insomnia.

Christianity is more than a religion; it is a personal relationship with God. We must not let the rules and regulations of religion get in the way of having a direct connection with Jesus. He is the Living God who hears and sees us, talks with us, and takes care of us. He is always near; His Holy Spirit comes to dwell in us after we surrender our lives to Him and make Him our Lord and Savior. He is in us, and we are in Him. Above all the other spiritual gifts God gives us, the Holy Spirit is the most precious and beautiful gift! Not only do we get to do life with Jesus on Earth via His Holy Spirit, but we also get to spend our Eternal Life with Him in heaven.

All heavenly power belongs to Jesus, as He is the Lord of lords, King of kings, and God of gods! He died for you and me and for all humanity on the Cross, so we would be saved from eternal torment, be healed of our sicknesses and diseases, and be delivered from our sins. If you want to receive your freedom and healing from Jesus, then invite Him into your heart, repent of your sins, and ask for His forgiveness. You can say a simple prayer of salvation such as the one below.

> *"Father, I know that I have broken your laws and my sins have separated me from you. I am truly sorry, and now I want to turn away from my past sinful life toward you. Please forgive me and help me avoid sinning again. I believe that your son, Jesus Christ, died for my sins, was resurrected from the dead, is alive, and hears my prayer. I invite Jesus to become the Lord of my life, to rule and reign in my heart from this day forward. Please send your Holy Spirit to help me obey You, and to do Your will for the rest of my life. In Jesus' name I pray, Amen."* *

Jesus is the Supreme God. He loves you and knows what you have been going through, as nothing is hidden from Him. Jesus is waiting for you, and He looks forward to receiving you with open arms. Your life may not be easy, but He understands all of your struggles more than you can imagine. Don't let another moment of your life pass by without coming into the knowledge of Jesus, having a personal encounter with Him, and developing an intimate relationship with Him.

Philippians 2:9-11 (NIV)

>*"Therefore God exalted him to the highest place and gave him the name that is above every name, that at the name of Jesus every knee should bow, in heaven and on earth and under the earth, and every tongue acknowledge that Jesus Christ is Lord, to the glory of God the Father."*

What a WONDERFUL and POWERFUL name it is, the name of Jesus!

*URL: www.allaboutgod.com

About Mamta Mukerjee:

amta Mukerjee is, first and foremost, a lover of Jesus, and secondly a prayer warrior and "marketplace evangelist." She has a deep and intimate personal connection with the Holy Spirit. She fervently prays and ministers to ordinary people in ordinary places like grocery stores, coffee shops, libraries, shopping malls, restaurants and so on and expects God to move miraculously and mightily for them. Mamta does not shy away from sharing who Jesus is, the ONE True, Living, and Most High God, with others. Her passion for the Lord and compassion for lost souls motivates her to reach out to others and share the Good News of Christ.

Mamta is currently working on a second book, which will highlight the healing testimonies of those she loves and those she was led to meet in the "marketplace." You can follow Mamta's evangelistic and healing stories through the following online resources:

Website: www.mamtamukerjee.com
Instagram: https://www.instagram.com/ mighty.motivational/
Podcast: https://anchor.fm/mightymotivational-mamta
Facebook: https://www.facebook.com/MightyMotivational. with.Mamta

CPSIA information can be obtained
at www.ICGtesting.com
Printed in the USA
JSHW012318150723
44804JS00004B/60

9 781662 852671